The POWER *of* INCLUSION

The POWER *of* INCLUSION

Unlock the Potential and Productivity of Your Workforce

MICHAEL C. HYTER • JUDITH L. TURNOCK

WILEY

John Wiley & Sons Canada, Ltd.

Library and Archives Canada Cataloguing in Publication Data

Hyter, Michael
    The power of inclusion : unlock the potential and productivity of your workforce / Michael Hyter and Judith Turnock.

Includes index.
ISBN-13 978-0-470-83674-3

    1. Diversity in the workplace. I. Turnock, Judith L. II. Title.

HF5549.H97 2005   658.3'008   C2005-903374-6

Production Credits:
Cover design: Pat Loi
Interior text design: Natalia Burobina
Cartoon on page 21: © The New Yorker Collection 1996 Mort Gerberg from
    cartoonbank.com. All Rights Reserved.

Printer: Friesens Printing Ltd.

John Wiley & Sons Canada, Ltd.
6045 Freemont Blvd., Mississauga, Ontario L5R 4J3

Printed in Canada

3 4 5 6 7 FP 14 13 12 11 10

Table of Contents

Foreword

When I came to Gillette, I found a company with great strengths … and serious, but fixable, problems. A succession of unrealistic business objectives had driven decisions that resulted in lost market share, high costs and a general lack of organizational discipline and cohesion. To address these problems, I focused on a turnaround plan that had three parts: making the most of our resources to improve financial performance, building our great brands with superior marketing and bringing everything together through Functional Excellence.

Functional Excellence is a global initiative to achieve best-in-class capabilities and performance … at the lowest possible cost. Functional Excellence is also a powerful tool to evolve our culture by driving continuous change and improvement throughout our organization. To create Functional Excellence, we clearly articulated high standards of performance for employees at every level, and we held our people accountable to deliver to these standards.

I was introduced to Novations/J. Howard & Associates shortly after I arrived at Gillette, and they were an excellent resource as we developed an action plan for cultural change and reaffirmed our commitment to an inclusive, diverse workforce. Whether interacting with our senior leadership, training our managers or advising our affinity groups, Mike Hyter and his team provided strong support as we worked to create an organization that could deliver more and better ... with fewer, but more fully engaged, employees.

The approach taken by Novations/J. Howard & Associates to establish a "Culture of Development" is the subject of this book. Their message is practical and contains key insights for people at every organizational level. I am confident that their fresh thinking will be a great guide for any organization that aims to activate talent, promote an inclusive workplace and achieve high levels of performance.

James M. Kilts
Chairman, President and Chief Executive Officer
The Gillette Company

Acknowledgments

This book, and indeed all the work of NJHA (formerly J. Howard & Associates), is possible only because of the research and writing of our founder, Jeff Howard. His ground-breaking work in capacity building spans more than three decades, in business as well as in educational and not-for-profit settings. His work with thousands of Efficacy graduates and hundreds of client companies continues to inspire all of us. We honor and respect his unique intelligence, his firm commitment and his leadership.

We have learned from every one of the hundreds of NJHA client companies over our thirty-year history, from their leaders and the many managers and others who have worked with us in private and group meetings, trainings, surveys and focus groups. For this book, however, a number of leaders gave generously of their time to share specific insights and experiences in extensive interviews: Valencia Adams, Carlos Perea and Elba Carrizo, BellSouth; Arthur Friedson, CDW; Robert Spencer, Entergy; Louis LaGuardia and Angel Rodriguez, FritoLay; Ned Guillet, Joseph Dooley and James White, Gillette; Toni Riccardi, PriceWaterhouseCoopers; Lee Merritts, Procter & Gamble; Sylvester

Mendoza, Quest Diagnostics; Gerri Rocker, Ryder Systems; Patricia A. Bussey, Sara Lee; Lisa Stewart, Shell Oil; Dan Casperson, Target; Faye Wilson, The Home Depot; Carlton Yearwood, Waste Management, Inc.; Henry Becton, WGBH; Juan Carlos Linares, DBM Colombia; Louis de Ocejo, Orchehill Associates; Michael Underhill. There is no doubt that their contributions to this book bring the theories to life, and their courage as change agents is why we persevere.

To the thousands of graduates of NJHA Efficacy Seminars who have returned to work with new confidence and renewed determination, we take this opportunity to applaud publicly your intelligence, hard work and determination. You have all helped your companies and your fellow workers to understand the benefits of inclusion, making the way a little easier for everyone who comes after you. A special thank you goes to those who shared experiences specifically for this book: Deborah Ashton, Maxine Bridge, Angela Brooks, Gil de las Alas, Hilary Keating, Jac Graves, Donna Brooks Lucas, Melvin McArthur, Gita Patel, Raymundo Quizon and Rochelle Stockett.

In addition, the people of NJHA are living examples of the dedicated and creative employees we hope to see developed throughout corporate America. The starting point is Naomi Sutherland, who managed the complicated process of getting us all to the finish line. Here is the team, those who have worked with us well past quitting time over the last three years to bring together all the resources necessary to make this book a reality: Perry Alter (Novations SDC), Mignonne Anderson, Audra Bohannon, Bruce Bramlett, Adriana Buendia, Daniella Capolino, Jorge Farias, Pat FitzGerald, Verna Ford, Cheryl Huddleston, Diane Johnson, Kathy Lenox, Gerry Lupacchino, Debra Luckett, Tom McKinnon, Nathan Nichols, Jim Rogers, Mace Vaughan, Ervin Walker and Shaunda Wilson.

Finally, our deep gratitude goes to Maureen Giovannini, whose countless hours of research, writing and editing have made this book immeasurably better than it ever could have been without her.

THE BUSINESS IMPERATIVE

My 30 years in business and my 23 years at P&G have convinced me that a diverse organization will out-think, out-innovate, and out-perform a homogeneous organization every single time.

A.G. Lafley, CEO
Procter & Gamble, Inc.

In today's business world, where technology advances rapidly and raw materials are globally available, the quality of each employee's performance is often all that differentiates companies' products. Increasingly, employees, and their willingness to devote their best efforts to the business objectives of their organization, represent the key competitive advantage. To be the best, companies need all employees—from hourly workers to senior leaders—firing on all cylinders, maximizing their individual potential *and* their contribution to the business.

Do corporations provide an environment where all employees are encouraged to "fire on all cylinders"? We find the opposite is more often the case. Human resource potential is actually wasted every day. In fact, even though CEOs we know agree that one of their biggest challenges is finding and keeping the highly qualified people they need for continuing business success, their companies continue to view existing employees as costs that can and should be reduced, rather than as the appreciable assets they are.

Business leaders are certainly well aware that any form of waste diminishes profitability and growth, yet waste of human resource potential continually occurs with relatively little attention or concern. What's wrong?

We believe this waste continues unchecked and unexamined because most people, including corporate executives, operate from a narrow, socially ingrained belief that talent and ability are unequally distributed among the population. If "some have it, and some don't," as the belief goes, people come into any organization with varying degrees of innate ability, and those with talent or merit are the ones who will succeed. Decisions about ability are made as early as recruitment, and often stay with individuals for as long as they remain with an organization. The widespread tendency, then, is for managers, from executives on down, to focus their attention on those select few deemed "high potentials."

Without intending to be exclusionary, managers shower the select few with development opportunities and support as they learn, perform and achieve success. Instead of recognizing this path to success as a self-fulfilling prophecy, managers step back and say, "Look how successful they are! We were right!" But what about the vast majority of other employees who have been ignored? In most cases they are less productive and less successful. Do managers see the performance gap as an outcome their behavior helped to bring about, behavior that stems from their beliefs about innate ability? Not very often. Since the shared assumption is "some have it and some don't," what happens to the select few and to the vast majority seems only natural, only to be expected.

This "sort and select" pattern serves to reinforce the belief among many managers and leaders that their organization is a meritocracy where the best naturally rise to the top. We consistently hear senior-level executives describe their human resource policies and practices as fair and open, where talented people who work hard succeed. Correspondingly, the formal policies and informal practices that focus on a select few are simply accepted as good business practices, without ever considering whether they might be contributing to waste of human resources. This view is understandable. Successful people quite reasonably believe that the process that resulted in their success is fair and based on merit.

Yet employees across those same organizations consistently express a different perception. They see opportunities for achievement given to a special few at the expense of most others. We find in survey after survey that most employees below the senior-manager level do not believe that merit determines who gets ahead. We frequently ask for reactions to the following statement: "In this organization, 'who you know' is often more important than 'what you know' for advancement." We find general agreement across all organizations and all employee groups, and it is one of the most consistently negative responses in our database. Some portion of these responses can be dismissed as sour grapes, but when there is such unanimity, there is at least an issue to investigate.

When we look beyond the survey responses in focus groups, personal stories reveal a downward spiral of declining enthusiasm and motivation, as employees become aware that only a few are recognized and nurtured in their desire to succeed and their efforts to contribute.

A NEW PARADIGM

Our book challenges the underlying belief that only some employees have the potential to be highly productive contributors. Instead, we propose an inclusive model of development and corresponding management practices based on a radically different paradigm:

> *In most companies, who succeeds and who doesn't is the result of an observable, repeatable process of development rather than innate ability. Through an inclusive approach to development that provides all employees with the opportunities usually reserved for a select few, organizations could maximize potential and productivity.*

This paradigm reflects our experience in all types of organizations. We have found again and again that those who succeed actually acquire their "talent" or "merit" because of the development attention they receive. They are given "stretch" assignments that allow them to develop skills critical to the company's business objectives, and during those assignments they are supported with guidance and encouragement. Their successes are rewarded with more stretch assignments, along with more encouragement and more guidance. And, most significantly, their difficulties, missteps and even outright failures are seen as learning experiences, calling not for dismissal but for more encouragement and guidance. These successful few benefit from an observable, repeatable process of development, and we would like to see that process made available to all employees.

Before you dismiss our goal as unrealistic, especially in this age of downsizing and restructuring, let us emphasize that we do not equate *development* with *advancement*. It is neither realistic nor feasible for a company to have every employee on a track to the top of the organizational ladder, or even a management-level position. At the same time, we strongly believe there is untapped potential in all employees, and developing all of them through the leadership, managerial and human resources policies and practices we propose in this book would exponentially increase the number of engaged, valued employees who have the knowledge, skills and opportunities to contribute to organizational success.

In a service economy, every employee's contribution matters, so we find the need for development at all levels of an organization, not just among the senior leaders. Think of a file clerk who doesn't understand the critical importance of storing a document where it can be easily retrieved in the future; valuable professional time can be spent trying to locate it. Think of the company receptionist who takes no personal interest in visitors or the retail clerk who does not pay attention to customer needs and wants; service business can be won or lost on such small factors. Ignoring those potential contributions is lost opportunity for the company—in business and in employee loyalty. It's no wonder the turnover rates are so high among entry-level employees.

Who are the people most often chosen for the development process? We find the choices are almost always influenced by the common human tendency for people to prefer others who are most "like" them. Of course, there are many definitions of *like*, but they typically begin with outward appearances. No one should feel guilty about this tendency; it is simply part of human nature, seen in all social groups throughout history, and it remains a powerful influence. It is therefore not surprising that in the West, where most leaders and managers have traditionally been white men, other groups find themselves at a disadvantage. In the rest of the world, it may not be white men at the helm, but we find a similar pattern of "like" people to the exclusion of most others. What happens to these disenfranchised groups is like what happens to canaries in the coal mine, who warn everyone else of imminent danger. Almost everyone will be excluded from the opportunities the select few receive.

THE FOUNDATION OF NOVATIONS'S SOLUTIONS

Our journey to these insights and the solutions originates in the Efficacy work pioneered by Dr. Jeffrey P. Howard over thirty years ago. Howard, an African-American, entered Harvard in 1966, when the school had just begun to admit students of color. During his four years as an undergraduate, he noticed that other African-American students, although the "best and the brightest" in their respective high schools, appeared to be much less engaged in learning than their white counterparts were or than they themselves used to be. Instead of spending long hours in the library, they would "hang out" in the cafeteria after meals or in each other's rooms. Howard wondered, how could they possibly succeed academically? At the end of his senior year, Howard got the answer he feared: the African-American students' GPAs were lower in all areas than those of white students. He determined to find a way to reverse the trend.

Because Howard posed his question at the same time Arthur Jensen attempted to prove, in the *Harvard Educational Review*, that most intelligence was genetically based, his determination to find an alternative took courage. His college-age courage was the focus of his doctoral dissertation in Social Psychology at Harvard, but it grew into a life-long quest to understand why African-Americans and other disenfranchised groups tended to underperform in certain academic and career settings, and to change those outcomes.

Through his Efficacy Workshops, where participants learn to apply effective effort geared toward bringing about a specific outcome, Howard has proved that development is based on a formula of effort and confidence, that the process of development can be learned, and that effective effort in the face of adverse conditions results in strong performance and greater self-confidence. The first experiments with his theory of development were with Harvard black undergraduate students for his dissertation, and all of them experienced greatly improved GPAs. The organization that bears his name, J. Howard & Associates, now Novations, was formed in 1977 to apply the theory to work performance. JH&A immediately became the leader in promoting the development of disenfranchised professionals. Over time, we have come to realize that almost all employees can benefit from Efficacy training.

Howard's approach is unique because it addresses both the logical and the emotional side of what it takes to maximize performance—for everyone. What began with his vision has grown through JH&A into a vast body of experience and learning. This book is our way of sharing the message with as many people as possible.

EARLY JH&A EXPERIENCE

In the early JH&A years, Efficacy inspired women and people of color to develop their potential and achieve success in corporate America. With our mantra, "It's not the stimulus, it's the response," we coached women and people of color to understand that by mastering their response to negative stimuli, however subtle, they could excel in their work environments. We challenged women and people of color—one by one—to increase their self-confidence, take personal responsibility for their development and become valued contributors. This early work was personally and professionally satisfying, and we inspired many people to envision and achieve greater career success. Those successes underscored the power of Efficacy: building confidence and applying effective effort to take charge of one's own career.

As time went on, however, we realized we were only addressing half the equation. Our work was changing individuals, but the organizations they worked for remained the same. From company to company, we heard the same stories over and over: renewed confidence and effective effort are not enough for success. There were also organizational barriers which most individuals were not able to overcome. These subtle exclusionary barriers were built into leadership, management and human resources practices, and they perpetuated unequal opportunity. Moreover, once we mapped the patterns, we realized their impact was not limited to women and people of color. Many, if not most, employees were stopped by those same barriers.

INCLUSION FOR EVERYONE

Today we focus on working with corporations to eliminate those exclusionary practices. We help companies maximize the performance potential of every employee, because doing so will maximize company performance overall. This book, therefore, is not a diversity treatise about the exclusion of women and people of color; it is about the inclusion of all employees. However, we strongly believe that the treatment of women and people of color serves as an important barometer of the extent to which an organization is committed to building and sustaining a truly inclusive environment. While this book focuses on company policies and management practices that affect all employees, whenever relevant we highlight the special challenges that women and people of color continue to face.

We propose a culture of development that will unlock everyone's potential, and replace the current business reality of wasted talent and lost productivity. Our Efficacy graduates are the bellwether for the majority of employees who are disengaged; they made their way as individuals, bucking the sort-and-select system in place at most companies, and everyone has benefited. How much better company performance would be if all employees were included in a culture of development! Of course, a culture of development does not exempt individual employees from taking personal responsibility for their careers. It simply means their development responsibility is now shared by managers whose job it is to encourage and support their efforts. Ultimately, by ensuring the development of all, we maximize company productivity, profitability and long-term business success.

The logic of the paradigm shift draws further support from increasing globalization. As companies operate in increasingly

diverse cultures, adopting inclusive management practices assumes greater importance, both for maximizing employee
productivity and for capturing market share. Our work with
companies outside the U.S. has convinced us that analogous
patterns of exclusion and preference operate universally: they
limit potential everywhere. The interventions we outline in this
book are relevant around the world.

WASTE OF POTENTIAL TALENT BEGINS AT FIRST CONTACT—AND CONTINUES

How does the natural tendency to select like candidates actually play out at work? We find that different development tracks
are established through very small actions even on the first day.
Picture two new team hires on the same day, both with equally
impressive educational qualifications and work experience. Let's
assume here that the manager is a white man, as would be the real
experience in U.S. corporations much of the time. To illustrate
the point about disparate treatment, let's assume one of the new
hires is a white man and the other is a white woman.

> *The manager welcomes the new man with a big smile
> and a firm handshake. "We've heard a lot about you,
> and I'm really looking forward to having you on the team.
> You've sold real estate and we sell computers—but sales
> is sales, and we know you won't slow down because the
> product is different. We can get you up to speed on our
> computers in no time. Say, how about having lunch with
> me today? I'll get a couple of the other guys to join us. We
> can talk about what you should start working on—maybe*

some of our new accounts. Based on your record, you'll hit the ground running, and we're ready to do everything we can to make that happen. My door is always open— don't hesitate to come in if you have a question."

Then the manager greets the new woman. His handshake is weaker, and he averts his eyes slightly. "I understand you've been assigned to work with us, and I want to welcome you to the company. I know that you've had some experience selling computers to government offices, but you'll learn that it's a different ball game here. Our customers are for-profit businesses, and it can be pretty rough-and-tumble working with them. We'll give you a couple of small accounts to start out with, and see how it goes. Our regular sales staff meeting is next Monday, so you'll be able to meet all the team members then. If you have any questions or problems, I'm usually in my office at the end of the day, so you can stop by then."

There is nothing technically wrong with the manager's behavior toward the woman. But when it is compared with his behavior toward the man, it becomes clear the manager has already made his decision about who has the talent, whether or not he is consciously aware of it. He has signaled his commitment to giving the new man the support he needs to become a high performer, from new accounts, to existing accounts, to guidance. And it really doesn't matter whether or not the two new hires are aware of the different treatment.

What about the new woman? She may have enough self-confidence and experience to be angry about her new manager's low expectations for her and to fight for sales numbers that will prove him wrong. But for many, the more likely response is to question their own ability: "He knows this business, and he seems to think I'm going to have trouble. Maybe he's right. There must be differences between selling to government and private companies that I don't understand. And he really doesn't want me to bother him with questions. I hope I can find another team member who will be willing to show me the ropes. This is going to be tougher than I thought."

It is possible that experience over time could prove either of the manager's initial assumptions wrong, but for most people those assumptions and the related behaviors will help create self-fulfilling prophecies. The new man is already positioned for success; he is innocent unless proven guilty. Further, it will be hard to prove him guilty, because any mistakes he makes will probably be interpreted as part of his learning process.

By comparison, the new woman is guilty unless or until she can prove her innocence, which is difficult if not impossible, and she has been left on her own. If she makes a mistake, she probably will not get a second chance, because any failure will be seen as proof that the manager's initial low expectations were correct.

Perhaps she can hustle enough to prove him wrong, but she will have to be careful about being labeled "too aggressive" in her efforts. It is now commonly understood that assertive behavior on the part of a man is viewed positively, while an assertive woman is viewed as inappropriately aggressive. In focus group after focus group, we find women professionals relate examples of this same disconnect.

There are endless varieties of these differing initial encounters, some more subtle than these examples and some even more obvious. This particular scenario simply illustrates how a manager's unconscious tendency to feel more comfortable with someone like him or her translates into assumptions and behaviors that set those mirror images on a path to development and success. The equally natural tendency to feel less comfortable with someone who is not like oneself sets others on the path to lowered performance.

If the differential treatment did not go beyond the initial contact, perhaps everyone could eventually get on an equal footing. Unfortunately, a manager's unconscious comfort or discomfort continues. It colors the assignments each person receives, as well as the support and guidance offered during completion of the assignment, and the resulting assessment of that person's performance. The truth is, successful people were not born talented. They received a pattern of preferential treatment, and it's the pattern that determines who is successful, and who is not.

Of course, there are always some people who succeed even without the special development attention. They have enough self-confidence and personal and professional ambition to demand opportunities and to deliver results. These people, however, are the exceptions, and we are concentrating on the rule. When we afford all people the same development attention that we give to those selected as the talented few, we discover a huge reservoir of untapped potential.

This is not to say that every employee is CEO material or would want to be CEO. Nor, as we emphasized earlier, does development necessarily have to lead to formal advancement. We encourage creating a work environment in which everyone is valued as capable of continuous learning and improvement, delivering the high performance that every company needs to remain competitive. Formal advancement and succession planning are different though related strategies, based on the leaders' assessment of the organizational structure that will best achieve the company's business objectives. A culture of development should produce most of the talent necessary to fill whatever roles a company decides are critical.

CHANGING DEMOGRAPHICS

When we view these patterns and practices in light of the vast demographic changes apparent now or projected for the U.S. workforce, we find an even more compelling business imperative. Today women represent almost half the workforce, and their numbers are expected to continue to increase. Now, in 2005, so-called minorities represent roughly a third of the population; within forty more years the majority, and their percentage in the workforce is rising accordingly. This shift also represents the continuing immigration of people from other parts of the world—for example, Central America, Mexico and Asia.

Efforts to open the doors of corporate America to "others," begun by black Americans and women in the 1960s, have resulted in dramatic diversity at lower levels. The demographic changes at work today will push diversity even further, as people of color represent a larger and larger percentage of the workforce. In less than a decade, women and people of color will represent almost 70 per cent of new entrants to the workforce. No company can survive if its work environment is not hospitable to the full range of people.

Another demographic shift with important implications for the workplace is increasing longevity. More and more people work well into their 60s, and many want to work into their 70s—for financial reasons as well as for personal satisfaction. We expect this trend to increase. What can and should companies do with these older employees? Simply wait for them to retire? Encourage them to retire by refusing to give them development opportunities and challenging assignments? Why would a company choose to forgo valuable contributions from employees with proven loyalty, dedication and ability?

It's a small analytical step to the realization that these demographic shifts also represent new customers. People of color in the U.S. alone now represent buying power in excess of $1.5 trillion, and that number will only increase as their numbers increase. Women are regularly found to be responsible for the bulk of family-spending decisions. Gays, lesbians, disabled people and senior citizens are increasingly well heeled, discerning and demanding customers. To remain competitive, companies need to understand the entire range of customers.

There is every reason to believe that the U.S. experience—the need to draw talent from a diverse labor market and the competition for customers from a diverse world market—will be mirrored throughout the world, as the global economy reaches every country, city, town and, eventually, village. The recently retired principal of a global financial firm calls inclusion "the price of admission for winning and sustaining new business," because even corporate customers are demanding it from the companies they do business with. It is probably a good time for corporate leaders to put some new thinking into "the normal course of business."

UNLEASHING THE POTENTIAL OF YOUR WORKFORCE

This book describes the strategic and operational shifts in processes that will create a culture of development capable of unleashing the potential of your workforce. Building this new inclusive culture of development does not require inventing a whole new system of people management. It just means shifting focus. Instead of concentrating development opportunities and support on a select few, we suggest companies give those same benefits to everyone. We have organized the book so readers can go directly to those chapters addressing their particular interest, perspective, expertise or challenge.

Chapter One, *Two Models of Development,* explores the two contrasting theories we find underpinning human resource development policies and procedures and the resulting development models. The first theory, alluded to earlier, what we call "Castes in Concrete," is what we believe has put us in the fix we are in today. This theory assumes that only some employees are talented. The resulting development model finds managers who "sort and select" among their direct reports, charged with identifying quickly the special few and then developing their "innate" potential.

We propose a different theory, one that leads to a very different development model. Our theory, that all employees have the capability to contribute to the important work of the corporation, leads to what we call the "capacity-building" model of development. Our model assumes that most employees will make valuable contributions if we engage them in an environment rich in realistic challenges, positive expectations and a focused and deliberate process of development. These key points are illustrated with concrete examples from our own professional experience, as well as examples from organizational leaders with whom we have worked.

Chapter Two, *Overcoming Barriers to Development: Eliminating Negative Treatment and Encouraging Quality Treatment,* demonstrates through examples that Quality Treatment or

Negative Treatment, not innate ability, result in varying levels of performance and productivity in the workplace. Managers' judgments about intelligence and negative reactions to differences can seriously affect people's learning, development and productivity. We explore the relationship between stereotypes and the way we treat people and then encourage readers to examine their own tendencies to judge and stereotype. How do those tendencies affect your own behavior as well as others' responses? What is the impact on work performance?

Chapter Three, *Managing Inclusion: Positioning All Employees for Success,* builds on the previous discussion of stereotypes, Quality Treatment and the need to understand one's own implicit assumptions. Understanding these concepts is an integral part of developing the inclusive "manager's mindset"—providing Quality Treatment to all employees. Showcasing the managerial skills that routinely position employees to develop their potential, we focus on managing a diverse population, all in the context of furthering the important business of the company. The inclusive manager sets goals with employees, coaches and mentors them, and then provides useful, timely feedback. We outline the transition that will bring the most value to the corporation—helping respected individual contributors learn to contribute through others without necessarily holding the title of manager. These specific skills and the manager's mindset are fundamental to the practical advice offered throughout this book.

Chapter Four, *Strategic Leadership: The Sine Qua Non of Change,* looks at the strategic role senior leaders play in bringing about the changes in organizational culture necessary to develop the potential of all employees. We lay out the business case and challenge leaders to make inclusion an integral part of the strategic business plan, with the resources, communication, measurable goals and accountability that accompany any successful company-wide initiative. We then discuss the need for senior leaders to break through the isolation that often keeps them from understanding what is really happening in the workplace on a daily basis. We also address the significance of leading by example, which includes grooming and selecting people representing diverse groups for key positions. Finally, we suggest that CEOs and senior leaders think about positioning their corporations for future competitiveness by leaving a legacy of employee development in addition to the more traditional legacy of business success.

Chapter Five, *Aligning Human Resources with a Culture of Development,* redefines human resources, moving it away from its traditional administrative and support role to the role of proactive strategic partner with leaders and line management. We identify five "critical points of contact" in an employee's work life, where company intervention can best inspire the desire to maximize one's potential for the good of the business: recruitment and selection, on-boarding, performance management, internal sourcing, both lateral and promotional, and succession planning. We also discuss how to coordinate these processes to achieve our three development touchstones: establishing the same high, clearly defined standards for all (beginning with the foundation of clear, consistent and widely communicated behavioral competencies); positioning all for stretch assignments; and providing honest, open and supportive feedback, so that each employee knows how to improve performance going forward.

Chapter Six, *Jump-starting Inclusion: Establishing the Infrastructure,* surveys the variety of strategies companies use to begin the process of integrating inclusion into the corporate culture—a Senior Inclusion Officer (SIO) in a stand-alone department, in HR, in legal or in strategic planning; executive steering committees; inclusion counsels; affinity groups; and mentoring—and discusses some best practices for each. At every step we emphasize our key recommendation: whatever the mix of programs and wherever the SIO stands in the organizational chart, (1) the position needs the weight and authority to influence key decisions, and (2) the officer appointed needs the skill, experience and sophistication to implement inclusion and a culture of development. It's a matter of influencing behavior change throughout a company, through leadership, policies, practices and continuous improvement.

Chapter Seven, *Inclusion in the Global Economy,* first looks at the transformation in business opportunities and challenges represented by the global economy and sets forth our value proposition: that attention to inclusion and a culture of development will improve global business outcomes. The principles and practices apply, whether companies are engaged in crossborder mergers and acquisitions, doing business through subsidiaries established in other countries or direct investments, or simply buying or selling products and services from or to other countries. We then share what we have learned from our initial experiences as consultants for companies engaged in the global economy and outline our process for achieving those results: make the business case, manage inclusion, enlist the support of local leaders and use human resources to facilitate and institutionalize the behavioral changes that support the best business performance.

Chapter Eight, *Measuring Progress and Demonstrating Results,* describes the critical roles of measurement and accountability in planning and implementing the organizational changes necessary to build an inclusive work environment. We know that what gets measured gets done, so we lay out a procedure for benchmarking where you are, discuss the process of behavioral change, and recommend four steps that lead to measurable, continuous improvement: setting realistic goals and designing effective interventions; establishing accountability and rewarding success; monitoring implementation practice; and documenting results.

* * *

We are all on a journey of discovery, engaged in continuous learning, so the experiences we relate here are by no means the last word. We have simply provided guidance for dealing with where we are today. We hope we will inspire you to create new ways of thinking and acting, new strategies and initiatives, because we firmly believe that inclusion and a culture of development will bring about the most satisfying professional experiences and the best business results.

CHAPTER ONE

Two Models of Development

"Miss Gaines, send in someone who reminds me of myself as a lad."

Our man in the cartoon voices the natural tendency we all have to prefer people who are most like us. This innate human reaction, coupled with an institutionalized set of assumptions about talent, has contributed to the unacceptable waste in human potential that we described in the Introduction. In this chapter we challenge these long-held beliefs about talent and development and replace them with a new set of assumptions that reflect our own experience as well as a growing body of scientific research.

THE HIDDEN POWER OF ASSUMPTIONS

Why bother with assumptions? Why not go directly to action? Management expert Peter Drucker explains why the assumptions that underpin organizational policies and practices related to the development of employees really do matter. "Assumptions decide what in a given discipline is being paid attention to and what is neglected or ignored." If the assumptions match reality, they are useful guides to effective behavior. But when they do not reflect what is true, they can lead us to wrong decisions. Therefore, if we want to make the best business decisions about people's capabilities, we have to look behind outward behavior to examine the assumptions that drive it, and then discard those assumptions that are wrong. Once we have established the correct assumptions, we can build the desired behavioral changes.

The stairway diagram in Figure 1.1 illustrates the step-by-step linkages we find between initial assumptions and business results.

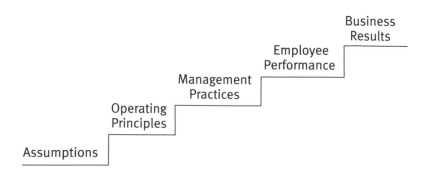

Figure 1.1: The Links between Assumptions and Business Results

THE "CASTES IN CONCRETE" MODEL OF DEVELOPMENT

Have you heard the old adage "Some have it and some don't"? This adage is shorthand for various ideas that fall under the assumption of "innate ability": people are born with certain intelligence levels, talents and abilities that define how much they will achieve in life. Within those confines, people can work hard and achieve more or less with their innate abilities, but the basics are there from birth. We refer to the "innate ability" way of thinking about human capabilities as "Castes in Concrete," to incorporate both the idea of the social class into which a person is born as well as the idea that what is cast in concrete is fixed and can never change.

We've all had experiences with the consequences of this "sort and select" approach, in processes designed to separate out those who are smarter, faster, better, and so on, into various castes. These labels are so pervasive in our society that they even begin at home before we get to school. One sibling is the smartest, another is the cleverest, the most charming, or the best athlete.

Then, when we get to school, we are quickly divided into groups based on ability. Whatever the groups are named, whether robins or sparrows, dogs or cats, we all knew even back then they really represented what we call the "very smarts" (VSs), the "sorta smarts" (Ss), and the "kinda dumbs" (KDs). We can all identify with these individual labels. For some, the groupings are liberating and inspiring; for others, they represent at best a challenge and at worst a "Castes in Concrete" ceiling. Those labels tend to follow us through life, and each of us knows which intelligence label we wear, and therefore which caste we belong to.

Although we undoubtedly know people who were labeled KDs and became successful anyway, we tend to explain those cases as exceptions that prove the rule. Such individuals may be viewed as "overachievers" or discussed in terms like, "It's amazing what she/he has been able to accomplish." We are all most likely to skip right over the possibility that the label might have been wrong in the first place.

Almost all human beings have an enormous capacity to learn. Ordinary people demonstrate that capacity by acquiring language at an early age and by "learning" many other highly complex tasks over the course of their lives. This does not mean all people have exactly the same amount of "intelligence," but it does mean most people have enough intelligence to contribute at very high levels.

Social psychologists have demonstrated the profound impact of "Castes in Concrete" thinking and practices on individual students. Psychologist Carol Dweck, for example, found in her school studies that students who believe "some have it and some don't" tend to approach life with what might be called a "proving orientation." This orientation, which starts from the assumption that a person is not perceived as capable and does not perceive him- or herself as capable, has two typical outward expressions. The first is refusal to try at all, perhaps the most common reaction. The second is more complex. Those who do get up the courage to try, spend much of their time proving to their teachers, parents and themselves that they are capable. There is no joy in learning because they have understood from an early age that public labeling and lower status await those designated as "not very smart." For them, no amount of success is able to change the initial assumption of not being capable. This orientation, then, puts students on a treadmill they can never jump off.

The effect of this "proving orientation" for all is debilitation of effort, and the effort decreases at a greater rate each time a student encounters failure or difficulty. Dweck describes this response to failure or difficulty as the "helpless" response. The children burdened with the "proving orientation" tend to give up more quickly and become apathetic, resisting challenging assignments because they hold a higher probability of failure. Ironically, by avoiding the assignments or projects they fear might cause them to feel less competent, they actually seal their fate. They never have the very experiences that would allow them to become better performers—those activities that would stretch them and make them more competent. If you don't engage in stretch activities, you will indeed never grow.

Because the "Castes in Concrete" model is so prevalent in society and in educational systems, it's hardly surprising that the same model finds its way into business and professional organizations. The "Castes in Concrete" assumption that "some have it and some don't" means the potential of many, if not most, employees is ignored. Here are what we find to be typical indications of organizations built on an exclusionary "Castes in Concrete" model of development.

Recruitment and Selection

Many organizations recruit only from certain schools and offer employment only to people above a target class rank. Others administer intelligence tests to applicants, with threshold scores determining selection. The goal of such practices is often explicitly stated—to employ only people of "proven ability." The assumptions behind these practices lead us at Novations to ask more questions. What exactly does "proven ability" mean in the work context, especially for those recent graduates interviewing for entry-level positions, with little or no work experience?

What do grades really prove? We have found grades to be a good measure of applied learning, but they may or may not be a good measure of capacity to learn. For example, grades can be a measure of teacher effectiveness or an indicator of where additional effort is needed by both teacher and student. And a student's ability to achieve high grades can correlate to life circumstances, not just the capacity to learn. Some students, including those who are judged to be the VSs, achieve high grades because they have adequate financial support and can focus on school assignments. Others may need to earn money in order to attend at all, and they must allocate their time to both paid work and completing graduation requirements.

Do the best grades in school prove ability to perform well at work? While many excellent students from top schools go on to perform well at work, we have also heard about many students who did not do as well in school but became star performers at work. Jack Welch was often heard to look for "somebody hungry," who was driven to succeed. We know of law firms or Wall Street investment banks with an informal requirement that recruits all represent a certain class rank at certain schools, even though a number of the firms' top money-earning partners do not fit that description.

The ability to balance conflicting priorities may also be more relevant to success in life, including at work, than grade point average alone. Think about the capacity to rebound from failure with an undaunted belief that "I can master this." Think about the capacity to exercise good judgment in taking moderate risks, discerning and using constructive feedback to improve performance.

Should "proven ability" be limited to having already performed well at the same kind of work? What about someone who has demonstrated the ability to come into a new situation and excel, for example, in combat, by moving to a different high school in a new location or bouncing back from the death of a close friend or relative? Or by being thrust into a leadership position without any warning or preparation and rising to the occasion? While the "proven" worker may be a safe bet, the best companies will want to identify workers who have demonstrated the desire to learn and grow and the willingness to expend maximum effort in any context, because they are most likely to be the source of the greatest productivity and the best new ideas.

Many companies use a technique called "behavioral interviewing" to gain insight into a candidate's capacity to learn and expend maximum effective effort. Companies first determine what behavioral competencies are critical to success in their organizations and then design questions for applicants that allow them to describe occasions in their lives where they demonstrated those competencies. Behavioral interviewing will be discussed further in Chapter 5.

Performance Management

"Castes in Concrete" thinkers are often comfortable with the "bell curve" to describe the distribution of human intelligence and other job-related abilities in a given population. The bell curve essentially posits that in any random group of people, their individual abilities would fall into three primary categories: 10 per cent in the lowest ranking, 10 per cent in the highest ranking, the 80 per cent in the middle plotted as a giant bell-shaped curve. Since "Castes in Concrete" thinkers tend to view performance as strongly

correlated with innate ability, many companies easily adapt the
theory to their annual performance evaluations: they demand
that the aggregation of evaluations represent a bell curve. A predetermined, fixed percentage of the population must receive the
highest and lowest ratings. Such "forced distribution" or "forced
ranking" systems have become an acceptable, even favored, performance evaluation tool. Such practices necessarily assume, we
believe wrongly, that only a small, predetermined fraction of employees can become top performers, and that a similar predetermined fraction of employees must be found unacceptable.

Potentials Ratings

If ability is "Castes in Concrete," when someone demonstrates capabilities (or reveals limitations), it becomes possible to predict
their future performance and their likelihood of being successful
at an organization. Many organizations actually codify this belief,
assigning employees numerical "potentials ratings," for example,
1 for high potential, 2 for medium or modest potential, and 3
for low. These ratings, when used, are usually assigned early in
anyone's tenure, in theory to give managers and HR guidance in
placement and assignments. Consider how one new manager responded after realizing the debilitating effects of the potentials
ratings:

> When I took over my new job the previous manager gave
> me a piece of paper with the names of all the 'reliable'
> people on one side and the 'slackers' on the other. Before
> I even met the team, he was dividing them up for me,
> and I didn't even question it. I handed out assignments
> accordingly and never even gave the 'slackers' a chance.

*Now when I go back, I'm going to do everything I can to
destroy that list.*

These labels once applied are difficult if not impossible to
overcome or change, even if an employee's performance demonstrates otherwise. Excellent performances in the case of 3s—or,
conversely, poor performances in the case of 1s—are explained as
aberrations. Not surprisingly, potentials ratings in most instances
are "Castes in Concrete."

Accelerated Development Programs and Rotational Assignments

Professional employees with high potentials ratings are often
placed on a "fast track," a series of relatively short and often rotating assignments in key segments of the organization. These
assignments are designed to expose high potentials to the most
important business departments as well as to the key company
leaders in order to position them as future leaders. Typically, these
strategic assignments rotate them through a series of managerial
roles and high-level individual contributor roles in planning, finance, operations, manufacturing, marketing and sales in order
to build a cross-functional breadth of knowledge, contacts and
skills. Those not put on the "fast track" are generally understood
to be out of the running for senior positions.

Employees' career trajectories can largely be plotted based on
these early judgments of ability and potential, and they are carefully controlled thereafter. Only those chosen for the fast track
are given the exposure and experiences that are the necessary
foundation for senior leadership positions.

Education and Training

Training also follows these same "Castes in Concrete" lines. Sort-and-select organizations invest heavily in training and development for those who are regarded as the high potentials—those equipped to benefit from the stretch opportunities. For the many others, some technical training may be provided, but seldom the developmental experiences that prepare individuals for greater responsibilities and more prestigious and visible assignments. The most valuable training opportunities are reserved for the select few.

IT WORKS FOR SOME

For those few people who have been selected as high potentials, the workplace implications of the "Castes in Concrete" model of development are by and large positive. From their initial contact with an organization—selection, hiring and on-boarding—whether applying for particular positions or recruited as interns, the labels indicate the treatment they are going to receive. They will receive most of their organization's development opportunities and support.

High potentials will receive the best job assignments—those that have high visibility and are linked to the company's key business objectives—the most encouragement and coaching support from their managers, the highest performance ratings, skills training on-site, invitations to seminars off-site, formal and informal leadership training, and formal and informal mentoring about how to be effective.

And many, if not most, high potentials rise to the occasion by excelling their stretch assignments. Why wouldn't they? They are encouraged, coached, mentored and groomed at every turn. We do not mean they are coddled. They are pressed hard, expected to hit extraordinarily high standards in relatively short periods of time. Their performance is tracked, and they are held accountable for their deliverables. We simply suggest that their hard work is immeasurably enhanced by the very high expectations and the quality support they receive. It's the conjunction of those factors—rather than some innate ability—that created their brilliant performance.

Ironically, when these high potentials are successful, the prevailing corporate rationale is that "Our system successfully targeted those with the most talent." But was it the original targeting? We think this question is premature, as premature as the potentials ratings.

Those high potentials indeed worked hard and long, gladly took on stretch assignments, knew they were being tested for greater opportunities, and they performed well. We do not suggest otherwise. But they benefited from a pattern of give-and-take between them and the organization; they worked hard and the company provided them with increasing rewards. These rewards inspired the confidence to stretch again and to achieve greater performance. The truth is that their excellent performance was the result of a give-and-take development process the organization affords its favorites; their success was a self-fulfilling prophecy. We call this "predicted performance" as opposed to "potential performance."

The real question for organizations is, how many other employees would have performed as well if they had been provided the same give-and-take development process? How many great performances are lost because the give-and-take development process is reserved for the select few? These questions relate directly to a company's ability to maximize the return on its payroll investment.

Perhaps the most important benefit of being among the high potentials is the treatment they receive when they encounter difficulty, failure or mistakes. An anonymous wise man once said, "An error does not become a mistake until you refuse to correct it." High potentials are the beneficiaries of that good advice. In most instances, their managers do not punish them for errors, and they do not lose their high-potential status. Instead, their managers encourage them to re-examine their strategies, learn from what went wrong, chart a new strategy based on the lessons they learned, and try again. They are, in essence, rewarded for taking calculated risks, their self-confidence remains high, and they continue to challenge themselves to achieve new improvements on behalf of the business and for their own professional growth. A well-known story about Tom Watson, founder of IBM, provides one such illustration.

> *A young junior executive had made a bad decision that cost the company $300,000. He was called into the CEO's office where the two of them spent considerable time reviewing the situation, the process used to make the decision, and how he might have reached a different and better decision. When the young executive was sent back to work and told to do things right the next time, he blurted out, "You mean you're not going to fire me?" Watson replied, "Fire you? I just spent $300,000 training you."*

In our view, if this same practice of using well-intentioned mistakes as opportunities for learning and improvement were extended to all employees, many more of them would become engaged and committed to learning, many more would grow steadily and increase their contributions to business success.

BUT MOST LOSE OUT

What do those assumptions mean for the many employees—most of the workforce—who are excluded from the high-potential group? In general, the organization invests little time or money in their learning and development. This makes sense, given the "Castes in Concrete" belief that their ability is fixed at a low level, and there is little anyone can do to change that fact. Needless to say, it is hard to maintain or develop self-confidence in the face of that kind of treatment. Most people who are labeled "sorta smart" or even "kinda dumb" eventually start to believe the messages about themselves.

Similar to Dweck's students with the proving orientation, these employees are unlikely to volunteer for risky new projects or assignments—the kind that stimulate learning—because they feel they must constantly demonstrate to their managers and to themselves that they are competent. Since mistakes or failure for them is regarded as proof of lack of intelligence and will limit their career possibilities, they avoid those risks at all costs. If they do get up the courage to try to stretch themselves, to take a risk, and then fail, their managers' responses contrast sharply with the responses to high potentials' failures. Instead of being encouraged to regroup and try again, they are told, "See, we were right. You don't have what it takes to succeed." Yet another self-fulfilling prophecy.

The "Castes in Concrete" model of development has a profound and negative impact on individual performance and therefore business results. The enhanced stairway diagram in Figure 1.2 incorporates the negative effect of that model of development at each step between assumptions and business results.

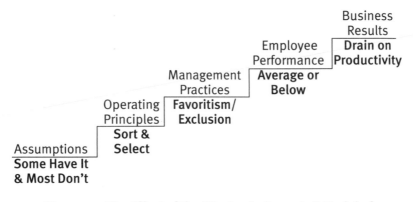

Figure 1.2: The Effect of the "Castes in Concrete" Model of Development on Business Results

Employees labeled "low potential" seldom have the opportunity to contribute to business success. Their lost potential is a business loss, even though it may be difficult to measure. Unfortunately, the lost potential can also result in harmful business performance that can be measured all too easily. One company's chief diversity officer describes how this happens.

Most people don't come to work to screw up, but those who feel left out often do, either unconsciously, because of depression or plain thoughtlessness, or consciously, because of 'malicious compliance.' We can expect similar results when highly educated people underperform. We have to engage our people just to minimize errors.

In today's service and knowledge economy, every position has the potential to impact the bottom line. Products can be duplicated, technology is constantly advancing, and access to raw products is virtually the same across the world, so people-based skills, such as quality and service, are the only reliable differentiation between companies. Your people represent your only compelling competitive advantage. If their potential is ignored, the loss can be significant. Only engaged employees are going to bring the continuous new ideas that lead to competitive advantage. The "Castes in Concrete" assumption and the debilitating orientation it fosters are therefore counterproductive. It continues to wield influence because it is taken for granted, customary and familiar—*the way we've always done things*—but this behavior hardly represents a solid business decision. There is a better, more rational and more productive way.

THE CAPACITY BUILDING MODEL OF DEVELOPMENT

The Capacity Building model is based on the demonstrable scientific reality that human beings, supported by policies and practices that encourage them to grow, are capable of continuous learning and development. One need only think about the process of infants learning language to realize that everyone has great potential: we all start from zero and yet learn to communicate effectively through speech in a matter of a few years. Even more astonishing is the fact that babies can begin to learn sign language at eight months of age.

Although we commonly talk about the extraordinary capacity of human beings to learn from birth to four years, a facility never equaled again, no one would seriously argue that human beings do not continue to learn throughout their lives, through elementary school, high school and college, on into adulthood, and even into old age. The learning process doesn't stop, especially when people receive support and feedback to encourage them to grow and when they put forth effective effort. Old dogs—and even old people—can learn new tricks!

Take a concrete situation that many of us are familiar with—learning to drive a stick shift. Everyone who has tried to master this skill started with stressful experiences including many mistakes, such as stalling in traffic—made worse by the beeping horns of irate drivers behind us. Some of us may have given up and reverted to driving with an automatic shift. But those who persevered—continued to practice, probably sought out feedback and coaching—got better. They learned to use their hands and feet to maneuver with ease in any traffic situation. While they were focusing on these physical activities, their brains were responding to the challenge by creating new mental circuits that enabled them to coordinate complex new skills. With enough practice, these skills became almost automatic.

Another example relates to the growing number of senior citizens who are taking advantage of computer classes—some geared especially to novices—to develop new skills. While some may not be interested in this or may wistfully say, "I'd like to learn but I'm too old," others take advantage of the skill building opportunities. Soon these senior citizens have developed the capacity to communicate with relatives and friends in new ways and even "surf the net" as part of their daily routine. Think also of the increasing number of senior citizens returning to college, and the number of countries and societies that depend on leaders who are well into their seventh or eighth decade.

Research in neuroscience has now confirmed what common sense has long understood. Practicing new and challenging tasks actually reorganizes people's brains cells (neurons) around new skills and capabilities and can even create new brain cells. Perhaps that is why many medical professionals urge people who are at risk for dementia or Alzheimer's or already experiencing the debilitating effects of those diseases to do crossword puzzles on a regular basis. If you ask your brain to work harder, you can actually become smarter!

The assumptions and practices that have developed from the success of those life-long learning experiences are the hallmarks of an inclusive organizational culture in which all employees have opportunities to build new skills. Employees there regularly perform at higher and higher levels. Here are some of the key features we find in organizations that have adopted the Capacity Building Model of Development as an integral part of their culture.

Recruitment and Selection

Managers focus on recruiting people with a penchant for learning, a readiness to accept challenges, flexibility in approaching problems and resilience in handling obstacles. This does not suggest that formal education is not important, but it does focus the discussion on what is most important about a credential: a personal commitment to learning.

"Behavioral interviewing" is a technique that allows the interviewer to delve deeper into a person's relevant experience, beyond having performed the same kind of work in the past. While past performance is indeed a strong indication of future performance, behavioral interviewing acknowledges that the desired performance can be demonstrated in any number of contexts. So questions are framed around specific behavioral competencies a company wants to recruit, develop and retain rather than around a specific job or title. Candidates are asked to provide examples of any circumstance in their lives where they have demonstrated the desired behaviors, for example, accepting challenges, showing flexibility, managing priorities and being resilient. These transferable skills are associated with leadership potential and are highly prized in a service and knowledge economy, at every job level.

Behavioral interviewing techniques have also helped interviewers hone their ability to be objective in interviews and assessments of candidates from diverse backgrounds. Without those techniques, diverse candidates were frequently described as not a good "fit." What does "fit" mean? It can mask myriad subjective criteria, conscious and unconscious. With these techniques, interviewers focus on concrete examples that demonstrate how and why a person doesn't fit. This analytical process has opened doors for many candidates who would previously have been summarily dismissed. We simply introduce behavioral interviewing here and discuss it more fully in Chapter 5.

Performance Management

HR policies take a non-traditional approach to evaluation, using a "criterion-referenced" system that judges performance against a standard of excellence and assumes every employee is capable of reaching that standard. This approach is diametrically opposed to the more typical "forced ranking" systems, which rank individuals against one another rather than against common standards or criteria, thus ensuring that only a few people will ever be rated top performers. A criterion-referenced system is inherently motivational, not only because it starts from the premise that everyone can hit a high standard, but also because it focuses attention on how to develop the skills and demonstrate the effort needed to meet that standard.

Accelerated Development

Accelerating development of skills and capabilities mandates broad distribution of special projects, task forces and other placements, including rotational assignments, that stimulate and demand new learning, rather than saving these opportunities for a select few. Common sense knows and research shows that motivation, innovation and performance often plateau when people stay in exactly the same job, doing much the same thing, for more than five years. Developmental assignments are platforms on which people can expand their skills through learning and get regularly "fired-up" by the challenge of new situations. Because they keep people engaged, they often are a deciding factor in a company's ability to retain key talent.

Rotational Assignments

Rotating assignments are very practical techniques to give a broad base of employees routine development opportunities. Most often they are lateral movement when promotion or advancement is not feasible. Employees may, for example, move from one location to another or move to a different aspect of similar work in the same or a different department. One could move from sales to marketing, or from one plant to another. In a large organization, the possibilities are endless.

Rotational assignments provide exposure to many different relationships and to other areas of an employee's function or operation, allowing an employee to put each activity into the context of the overall organization. In some cases these assignments tend to be very brief, designed primarily to give an employee additional orientation. In other cases, assignments are long enough for an employee to complete portions of a project or even an entire project. These longer assignments allow an employee to learn as well as to make an actual business contribution.

Promotion

Nowhere is the commitment to a culture of development more visible than in an organization's promotional practices. Many organizations routinely go outside when senior positions become available, but organizations committed to expanding the capacities of their people promote from within whenever feasible. Hewlett-Packard is one such company, and it is no coincidence that it has a turnover rate roughly one-third that of other Silicon Valley companies, where competition for those considered the most creative is fierce and constant.

Education and Training

It stands to reason that companies committed to mobilizing people toward learning and better performance will devote resources to providing education and training to all employees. Leading-edge training for all employees is a very expensive undertaking, and few if any companies approach the ideal. But we do know that every step toward the goal yields benefits, and each chapter in this book describes individual steps and strategies.

We have seen pockets of success at many companies. Most of you have probably worked for or heard about a manager who runs his or her department with the principles of the capacity building model of development in mind, people our founder and philosophical mentor Jeff Howard refers to generically as "the teacher in Room 222." Broad organizational change is simply the collective power of one-on-one changes. In fact, organizations like the Center for Creative Leadership and others who have studied development find that the most effective development for employees takes place on the job, and that learning is accelerated as a result of facing difficulty or failure, when feedback is available and applied to future performance.

Every company can decide to take those one-on-one steps. Start with your managers, asking them to identify developmental assignments in conversations with each of their direct reports. What interests those employees? Then urge them to coach those employees as they stretch, to offer support and guidance, and to give the constructive feedback that will encourage those direct reports to reach the next level of performance.

As company leaders, you can begin by identifying what you believe will be most important to your business over the next five years. What are the trends that will have the greatest impact? What are the products you will need to remain competitive? What are the new skills your employees will need to meet the new changes and challenges? What new resources will be necessary? When you have identified your business needs, you can tie your employee development strategies to those needs. That's just what you would be doing anyway; it just happens with an intensified purpose.

The matrix in Figure 1.3 captures the key differences in practice between the "Castes in Concrete" Model of Development and the Capacity Building Model of Development as they apply to each of the indicators we described above.

Figure 1.3: Comparing Practices under the Two Models of Development

	Castes in Concrete	Capacity Building
Recruitment	Selects candidates with proven ability	Selects candidates with capacity to learn and willingness to expend effort
Training	Delivers best training to best performance	Delivers best training to all employees
Evaluation	Forced-distribution systems group people in categories and fix expectations	Evaluation conducted with high standards and developmental objectives in mind
Potentials Rating	Potential for future performance rated high, medium or low, impacting decisions about future assignments	N/A
Rotational Assignments	"High potentials" given rotating assignments as part of "fast track" programs to prepare them for senior positions	Rotating assignments given to broad base of employees as routine part of development process
Promotion	Promotes high potentials" at a rapid clip; often fills top positions with outsiders	Explicit objective to develop broad base of employees; promotes from within

A capacity building mindset is the foundation for a culture of development that goes beyond human resource strategies and pervades the whole organization. The mindset begins at the top, with leaders who make it clear that they are committed to an ethic that expands capacities, then model this behavior in their own practices.

Similarly, management practices at all levels will concentrate on continuous learning and continuous improvements, encouraging all employees to take controlled risks on behalf of the company's business objectives. Finding themselves in a positive environment, employees will want to put forth their best efforts and engage their minds. Each stretch will build their confidence and encourage more effort. The result? Performance that consistently exceeds expectations. The enhanced stairway diagram in Figure 1.4 incorporates the positive effect of a culture of development at each step between assumptions and business results.

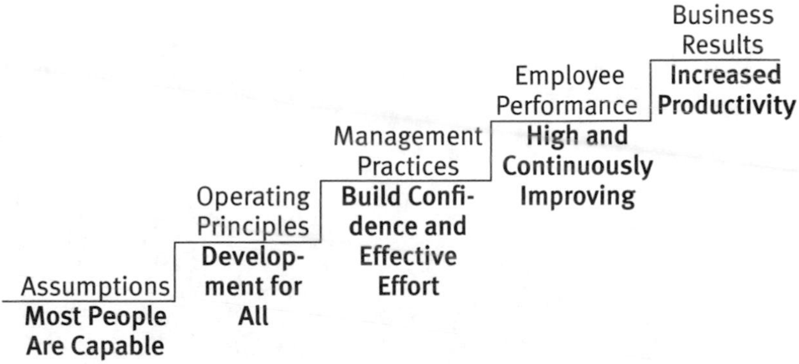

Figure 1.4: The Effect of the Capacity Building Model of Development on Business Results

With many more employees developing their potential and exceeding expectations on a regular basis, companies will continuously improve their products and services, thus gaining a competitive edge.

The benefits of building an inclusive organization characterized by a culture of development are numerous and, in our experience, well worth the effort. At the same time, the journey leading to this goal is not without obstacles. In the next chapter we examine some common obstacles that organizations are likely to face and then offer strategies for overcoming them.

CHAPTER TWO

Overcoming Barriers to Development

Eliminating Negative Treatment and Encouraging Quality Treatment

Imagine if every employee were really engaged. There'd be no stopping that company.

Communications Manager

In the previous chapter and the Introduction, we argued in favor of an inclusive model of development that would benefit organizations by building the capacity, and thus increasing the business contributions, of *all* employees rather than a select few. In this chapter we examine more closely some of the barriers to inclusive development and then discuss effective ways to overcome them. These barriers begin with the fact that we—as human be-ings—all respond most positively to people like ourselves. Oth-er stumbling blocks to development include forms of Negative Treatment based on negative assumptions about an individual's capability. These barriers and negative assumptions affect those making business judgments about others as well as those being judged.

NEGATIVE TREATMENT

We use the term Negative Treatment as shorthand for all the ex-clusionary tendencies that keep employees from achieving their best performance. To banish it, however, we first need to examine it closely. We define Negative Treatment very specifically as:

- unconstructive interaction or behavior,
- conscious or unconscious,
- directed toward an individual,
- ranging from condescension or indifference to outright hos-tility and aggression.

If we just think about the common meaning of the two words, it should be obvious that Negative Treatment is not a hallmark of great management; such treatment would seldom if ever promote excellent performance, and is therefore not in the best interest of any company. But to banish it, we first need to examine it more closely. It helps us to look first at the kind of positive interac-tions the select few receive, and then to think about the other side of the coin. In Negative Treatment, the interactions are discour-aging, unhelpful, curt or grudging, and, even worse, there may be no interactions; people may be completely ignored.

Though we may not often think about it, most of us would realize that Negative Treatment is likely to have an unfavorable impact not only on feelings, thoughts and behavior, but also on work performance. We all know that most of us, even the most self-confident, are sensitive to what we consider Negative Treatment, and each of us can probably remember an incident where harsh words about our ability rattled our confidence. Think back to your own years in school. One former executive, for example, still remembers vividly a principal's negative assessment of her ability:

> When I was in eighth grade, the principal told me I was not college material, and I should forget about the scholastic programs and stay in home economics and sewing. I was in tears because my dream was always to go to college. My mother, who was in education herself, got me back in the academic program, but that principal had a lasting impact on me.

This person overcame the Negative Treatment and went on to become a public relations executive at a major firm and a board member of several small for-profit companies before starting her own business. For most people, however, it can be hard to get back on track and stay there. Most of us benefit from outside help, and, as we will see, providing that kind of guidance is a key characteristic of the best managers.

Figure 2.1 depicts the causes and effects of Negative Treatment as we have defined it. The effects are individual as well as collective, because diminished productivity means a diminished business bottom line.

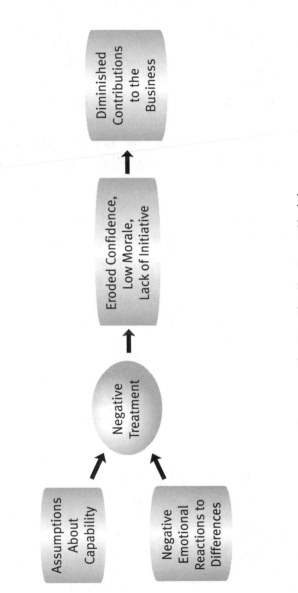

Figure 2.1: The Negative Treatment Model

RECOGNIZING NEGATIVE TREATMENT IN YOURSELF AND OTHERS

How do managers recognize Negative Treatment in the workplace, either in themselves or in others? Here is what three managers we work with said about their newfound insights about their own behavior.

This past year when I read my 360 survey results and saw the negative comments from the people who work for me, I was blown away. I felt a little defensive at first, but fortunately for everyone, including me, I saw the light. In less than a year my people were telling a different story, because now I make sure I talk to them, ask their opinions, give them chances to develop—if it's something I can't do for them myself, I find someone who can. We've all accomplished so much more.

I always had my few "stars," the people whom I knew I could count on. When my mentor cahllenged me about only relying on the same few, I countered by saying I didn't have time to "develop" the others. Then he asked me how much time I would save if all my people were performing at higher levels. I thought about that and began to make time to give others more opportunities and coaching. It's really paid off!

I went home that night and made a list of my "go-to's," and they were all male and all white, just like me, and how much I valued each was in direct proportion

*to how long I'd known them. How could I have been so
predictable! I didn't just vow to increase the number and
diversity of my "go-to" people. I went back the next day
and told everybody what I'd realized. I felt bad about my
report and what it said about what I'd done—or hadn't
done—but I was also pretty sure I wasn't the only one.*

Once managers understand the Negative Treatment lens—
how to question your own assumptions and those of others, how
to move beyond "the way we do things around here"—change
can begin.

Sometimes Negative Treatment is easy to spot. One marketing manager we know remembers the treatment she received
from her boss when her marketing initiative failed to live up to
his expectations.

*Our store promotion had not gotten the numbers we
anticipated, mostly because the economy was down, but
my manager sent me a very stormy email blaming me,
with copies to many people whose good opinion I valued.
I was so angry, because I had worked very hard on the
promotion, and I wanted to fire back at him. Fortunately, I
waited until I had calmed down. I took the high road and
simply responded with my plans for the next quarter.*

It would be convenient if all instances of Negative Treatment
were as obvious as this case, but most examples today are subtle
and often occur outside the manager's view. The vignette we described in the Introduction, about how a manager treated two
new employees, one white male like himself and the other a white
female, is a good example of the type of Negative Treatment that

takes place every day in organizations when managers, often unconsciously, act in ways that communicate their negative assessment of someone's value.

Take, for example, this story told to us by an African-American client.

> *I was asked to give an important presentation to a group of executives—all of whom were white. The presentation went very well. Following the presentation, one of the executives came up to tell me that I did a great job, adding, "I was really surprised that you were so articulate."*

In today's workplace, many organizations have formal "Zero Tolerance" policies designed to reduce the most offensive manifestations of Negative Treatment. But subtle forms are still common, and overt forms, particularly with regard to sexist jokes, are still tolerated and even condoned. Sometimes the symptom you see is anger, but most reactions are more muted. Unfortunately, many respond by accepting the perceived low expectations. These negative self-images manifest themselves in:

- diminished performance ("I'm not going to do any more than just enough to get by"),
- reduced motivation and creativity ("I'm certainly not going to share any of my ideas"),
- loss of confidence ("I knew I couldn't do it"), and
- disengagement from the work and from co-workers ("I'm never going to ask for anything from anybody").

Of course, managers who see this behavior feel justified in their negative judgments about the individual—which in turn engenders more Negative Treatment, and an unsatisfactory downward spiral gets put in place. More Negative Treatment leads to

more unproductive performance and more Negative Treatment.
The key to unraveling this spiral is to stop it before it gets started.
We'll talk more about how to do that later in this chapter, but
the first step is to train yourself to see the signals that Negative
Treatment might be occurring. Figure 2.2 gives examples of the
cues you can look for to identify and stop Negative Treatment before it has done the worst of its damage to the confidence, morale
and performance of its recipients.

Figure 2.2: Negative Treatment Cues

Negative Treatment Cues
Level of Respect/Value/Recognition

- Being ignored at meetings while others are regularly asked
  for their opinions
- Exclusion from meetings—even when concerning one's own
  projects
- Having ideas you express in meetings ignored or belittled
- Not receiving small signals of favor, such as training, confer-
  ences and out-of-town meetings
- Not being included in informal lunches or social activities
- Silence/lack of social pleasantries ("hello," "have a good
  weekend")
- Comments about the undesirability of working within a cer-
  tain group
- Expressions of surprise toward employees who don't fit
  stereotypical expectations ("pretty good for a woman")
- Derogatory/sexually inappropriate references and terms
- Stereotype-based or sexually loaded jokes

Development Opportunities/Support

- Not being told of other events, projects, trends or occurrences that have an impact on your project
- Receiving job/task assignments that reflect the organization's lower expectations for certain groups
- Not receiving assignments that are central to the company's core business
- Little or no feedback about the quality of one's work or areas for improvement
- Tendency to promote based on the potential of some individuals while others have to "prove themselves" first

Organizational Practices

- Demographics of work group out of alignment with local community or client base
- Discrepancies in upward mobility and retention rates among groups
- "Stacking" of certain groups in certain functions or at certain levels of the business
- Business facilities that reflect lower status for some groups (e.g. lack of wheel-chair access; inadequate bathroom or break room facilities; inappropriately sized equipment or uniforms)
- Recognition out of line with contribution (some people overlooked when team recognition given; lack of consideration for awards/perks)
- Corporate literature and advertising reflect only the traditional group
- Anger with/complaints about hiring/promotion policies

Who is most likely to receive Negative Treatment in the workplace? Again, the reverse image is an instructive starting point. Who is most likely to receive Positive Treatment? As the cartoon at the beginning of Chapter 1 suggests, those most likely to be viewed as talented and worthy of special good attention are those with whom managers are most comfortable—those who are most like them. It follows that those most likely to feel the brunt of assumptions of lesser capability and thus most likely to receive Negative Treatment are those with whom managers are least comfortable—those who are least like them.

What does "like" include, and what does it exclude? The similarities and differences begin with outward appearances—gender and race as well as age and disability. But other factors come into play as soon as there is further interaction: sexual orientation, religion, national or regional origin, language or experiential factors such as where you grew up, your educational background or what sports or other interests you share, as well as personality, style and temperament. Witness the direct animosity experienced by many Middle Eastern or Muslim employees as "immigrants" in Europe or as terrorist "suspects" in the U.S. Your career background can also lead to Negative Treatment, for example, if you worked for the company that was acquired, or something as simple as a production person moving into an engineering environment.

Even your personal style can elicit Negative Treatment. For example, think of how some people back away from someone who laughs a little too loudly or speaks too openly about her private life. One client who recently joined a Wall Street investment bank discovered her colleagues enjoyed mocking her relatively slow walk in an environment where everyone took pride in moving fast—literally and figuratively. Someone finally explained to her, "Anyone who walks that slow will never be taken seriously around here."

In some cases, relying on outward appearances alone to assume someone's position on issues is a risky strategy. A sales associate we know, a white woman, often heard her colleagues making jokes about black customers when they were on breaks, assuming she would agree with them. What her colleagues did not know was that she had a black son-in-law of whom she was very fond. As the sole woman in her group, she felt uncomfortable challenging the banter or even saying she didn't like it. She never felt truly comfortable with her colleagues, and her company's tolerance of their behavior made her uncomfortable about the workplace in general. Of course, white people don't need to have a black relative to be offended by such behavior, but it is often a personal connection that allows us to realize the pain caused by jokes that we previously ignored or considered harmless teasing.

Another white woman we know who attended a black law school was horrified to find recruiters from a major law firm joking with her about how ill prepared the black students they had interviewed were. This woman expressed her disagreement, and the invitation to come to the firm for a day-long series of interviews was withdrawn.

A gay client shared the stress of trying to hide his sexual orientation in an environment where he knew he could not be open.

I cringe every time I hear a gay joke or comment about "fags." It makes me leave my identity at the door when I walk into work every day, and that's hard. People keep asking me about my social life, and I know they're curious

why I never talk about it with the other guys. I'd like to get
a job with a company where I wouldn't be afraid to "come
out," but until that happens I just keep hoping no one
finds out. It's really hard to stay focused on the work I'm
supposed to be doing.

Are the jokes and questions about his social life innocent, or
are they really designed to make him uncomfortable? Regardless
of the intention, the result is the very definition of a hostile work
environment, and the personal price is stress and decreased productivity.

As different as these examples of Negative Treatment may appear, they all share a common result: diminished engagement on
the job. And the negative impact does not stop with the individual recipient. Each person's diminished productivity diminishes
the company's bottom line.

STEREOTYPES

What is really behind Negative Treatment? For most of us, pervasive stereotypes in our society are the source of much of the
Negative Treatment that occurs. We all share a natural tendency
to sort and categorize the many experiences we have daily, and
we have all been socialized to some degree to rely on certain stereotypical responses. We find some of those stereotypes, however,
to be common forms of Negative Treatment. We seek to counter
stereotypes, which we define as:

- a commonly held, usually negative, assumption about a group
  of people,
- based not upon an individual person, but upon perceptions
  about the group to which that person belongs.

Because stereotypes reside in our subconscious, they exist whether or not we are aware of them or even consciously believe them to be true. They represent a kind of unconscious programming that drives our thoughts and behaviors. The real problem with stereotypes is that, by focusing on a group rather than on individuals, they often prevent us from obtaining real information about the feelings, skills, experiences or capabilities of another individual. If we base our perceptions on the stereotype, we may mistakenly assume that we already have all the information we need about someone who is "different." But we need more reliable information to make the best decisions for the business.

For example, when dealing with women, many managers have a difficult time forgetting perceptions of women as weaker, more emotional and less dependable, at least at work, because they put family obligations ahead of their careers. These perceptions may reside at an unconscious level, whether or not experience justifies them. Making the task more difficult is the fact that it is still socially acceptable to ridicule women. A 2004 survey of workplaces found that more than a third of employees had heard sexually inappropriate comments during that year. While the percentage of other inappropriate comments continues to decline, women are still expected to tolerate blatant discrimination, which we as a society label "harmless teasing." And this survey does not begin to address or measure the unconscious negative assumptions that drive the outward behavior.

The burden of stereotypes has been and remains especially heavy in the United States for blacks, but in every country and every culture there are analogous situations. In Europe, "immigrant" is such a stereotype, in India the "untouchable" caste. And many women in countries around the world are still literally pieces of property. With regard to these identifiable groups of people in every culture, what Novations founder Jeff Howard calls "rumors of inferiority" still hold sway, no matter what we say or think we believe.

While fewer and fewer people actually say they believe some groups of people are intellectually inferior, the discredited belief remains pervasive. No matter what brain research has proved, theorists like Charles Murray and Richard J. Herrnstein, who published *The Bell Curve* just over a decade ago in 1994, still convince large segments of the population that some groups of people are intellectually inferior. There are so many messages, spoken and unspoken, about stereotypes in our daily lives that the unconscious and even conscious beliefs and thoughts are difficult to eradicate, both for managers and for the subjects of the stereotyping.

Managers, along with everyone else, have to work hard to reach objective decisions in all cases.

How do stereotypes typically play out in the workplace? To begin with, they can fuel the assumption that all members of the group have less ability and lower qualifications. These "rumors of inferiority" are revealed in the statements of manager after manager, who, when asked about their views on diversity, say: "I'm in favor of diversity, as long as it doesn't mean lowering standards." It is similarly revealed in the words of a manager who headed his company's supplier diversity efforts: "We're really going to enhance our supplier diversity program, but we're not going to compromise quality."

Underlying each of these seemingly supportive statements is the belief that allowing suppliers not owned by white men to compete for the company's business runs the risk of using lesser standards and accepting lower quality. While the person expressing the concern is focusing on support for a company's supplier diversity program, those employees who are also representatives of diverse groups or who identify with them hear the negative connotation. It is hard for either "side" to understand the other.

One executive vice-president of human resources we work with managed to bridge the communication gap. Here's how he expressed what he learned.

> *The average white person hears that kind of comment and doesn't bat an eyelid. He says to himself, "That makes sense." But if an African-American or a woman hears it, they see the implication: going to a woman-owned or minority-owned business means there's a risk of lower quality. You never hear a manager say, "We're going to put the contract for plastic welding supply out for bid, but we're not going to compromise quality." I would have trouble picking up a subtle message like that, but it shows there's still that kind of thinking underneath. People think they're saying the right thing. They don't realize that's a little arrow wounding somebody. It's that less conscious kind of thing that happens more frequently now.*

These deeply rooted and often unconscious beliefs place an additional burden on members of stereotyped groups. They may adversely affect performance, or may be one important reason why disproportionately more women and people of color leave one organization for another, seeking a more inclusive culture. In the words of one black professional,

> *Having to work twice as hard as everyone else, while my promotions are still viewed by some as part of "meeting a quota," is too much baggage to carry. I'm actively*

looking around for a place where my contributions are acknowledged and valued.

We suggest a simple test to determine whether or not this reason may underlie some of the turnover within a particular group in your organization. Look at the distribution of performance "grades" and potential categories to see if there is a disproportionate number of those in the numeric minority in the lower categories, or a disproportionate number of those similar to the leaders in the top categories.

Stereotypes can also affect assessment of another individual's potential in ways that *seem* positive. For example, it is common for Asian-Americans to be pushed toward IT positions, even if they are more interested in other areas, such as marketing. Often this is because their managers assume that Asian-Americans are good at math and science and less competent or not suited for positions requiring creativity. The irony is that these managers probably believe they are doing something positive by giving their employees development opportunities that would further their IT success in the company. In reality the managers were unintentionally pigeonholing Asian-American employees.

Another example comes from a well-meaning manager who always said he was committed to work–life balance. But his underlying belief that women, not men, were responsible for that balance caused him never to offer work assignments involving travel to women with small children. Unfortunately for one ambitious and capable woman in his department who had two small children, all the best assignments involved overnight travel. After she had discerned the pattern in his assignments, she went to her boss. As he described it,

I was shocked when she came into my office and asked me why I wasn't giving her any of the plum assignments necessary for promotion. When I explained I assumed she, as a mother with young children, would not want the travel these assignments involved, she told me she had already worked out an arrangement with her husband and mother so she could continue on the "fast track."

Sometimes simple but direct communication solves the problem. But sometimes the stereotype is so deeply engrained that no amount of discussion will create enough understanding to move past it. These stereotypes can color perception of someone's performance, even when we believe our assessment is objective. One sales manager we know gave an example of the extreme strategies that have been necessary in some situations to jolt evaluators beyond stereotypes:

I've been told the New York Philharmonic never selected anyone female or black until they started holding blind auditions. They literally had to put a screen between the judges and the musician.

The screen didn't change the performance; it changed the judges' perceptions of the performance. The sales manager went on to say,

That's why I like doing business over the Internet. People pay attention to my work without any idea of what I look like.

These two women, the one with the two children who wanted traveling assignments and the one who prefers communicating by email, found strategies to counter the stereotypes; they had the courage to intervene on their own behalf. Such interventions are still necessary to blunt the impact of stereotypes, even at an unconscious level, on key decisions like recruitment, assignment of development opportunities, performance assessment and promotion, along with the waste of talent that results. Beyond the obvious impact of stereotyping on the individual recipients, who expends valuable energy countering the stereotype that would otherwise be devoted to the work, think also of the resulting lost productivity to the company overall.

ELIMINATING NEGATIVE TREATMENT

With stereotyping and the Negative Treatment it so often precipitates so pervasive and so subtle, what can companies possibly do to eliminate it? There is no magic bullet, but we have found our six-step process, played out department by department, through each manager, works. It is not difficult or complicated to understand, but accomplishing it takes a great deal of commitment and patience. Managers begin by looking for the circumstantial evidence and then consciously working to unmask it and to convince everyone that it is counterproductive to business objectives.

1. **Observe your people and how they interact.** Look for overt evidence of Negative Treatment as well as reactive signs from recipients that may indicate they have been subjected to Negative Treatment. Some of the most typical reactions are a decrease in performance ratings, less enthusiasm, isolation, problems with productivity and/or anger and hostility. Let

your employees know your door is always open to discuss any issues or problems they may be having as the objects of Negative Treatment. We realize this is easy to say but takes a great deal of time and patience to accomplish. Recipients of Negative Treatment quite reasonably view coming forward with specific information as fraught with danger—those who have done so run the risk of being labeled "petty," "too sensitive" and worse; some have lost their jobs. Too often clients still tell us "there is no safe place to go" to express their concerns and find help to deal with Negative Treatment. It will take time for managers to change this unproductive dynamic.

2. **Don't rush to conclusions.** Take a strategic approach to exploring the issues: What exactly is going on? What's the history of the behavior problems you observe? Who seems to be involved? What seems to be causing the problems? It may take some time to sort through the evidence and then trace back to the causes, and many of your initial beliefs and assumptions may prove to be misguided. But you need very specific data. You cannot solve the problem without a deep understanding of the causes, the actual Negative Treatment and the results, especially where you are dealing with subtle or even unconscious influences. More important, without a clear analysis, you will be unable to convince any of your employees of the business cost of the problem.

3. **If you find Negative Treatment—and it would be an unusual office where you did not—make a concerted effort to get rid of it.** Call your employees together and state your firm belief: the productivity of our team—and therefore our value to the company—depends on all of us being focused on

the company's business objectives. Further, make it clear that each one's personal value to the team depends on his or her consistent and genuine ability to support the development of each of the others. In this positive and reinforcing environment, the team and each individual will achieve more. You may want to add that you believe everyone's personal job satisfaction will also increase. This step involves in-depth discussions about Negative Treatment.

4. **Talk specifically about the harsher impact of Negative Treatment on women and people of color.** Although anyone can be the object of Negative Treatment, your observations will probably reveal that it is more often directed against members of diverse groups, especially women and people of color. Older workers or disabled workers, for example, may not be included in all the informal office interactions, but these subtle forms of Negative Treatment are not as likely to have a negative impact on their work assignments or performance. This is where the slippery line between good-natured teasing among colleagues and debilitating Negative Treatment must be drawn clearly.

   Because women and people of color tend to be the canaries in the mine with regard to Negative Treatment—the first to succumb to the decrease in oxygen before an explosion, so they warn of what is imminent for everyone—we have found you will need to talk very specifically about their experiences and your commitment to ending their disparate impact. General language about fairness and opportunity for all is seldom enough because it allows too many people to skip over their own unconscious thoughts and feelings and the equally unconscious behavior—active or passive—those thoughts and feelings trigger. In addition, general language will probably not convince women and people of color that you understand and are comfortable discussing their specific challenges or that your campaign to eliminate Negative Treatment will necessarily include them. We all have to learn to stop walking on eggshells when it comes to discussing difference, but particularly on the issues of race and gender.

5. **Declare Negative Treatment off limits.** This is where leadership is paramount. Show commitment to eliminating Negative Treatment by behavior as well as words. Effective strategies include declaring your understanding and your goals in staff meetings and in informal talks among those who report to you. You can point out Negative Treatment when you see it, and you can mediate among employees when you observe reactions to it and discover the causes.

   We find rewards and punishments for Negative Treatment are effective strategies for jump-starting your campaign because they signal your serious commitment to hold everyone accountable. But those strategies alone lose their effectiveness over time because they also breed resentment, fear, anxiety, malicious compliance and cynicism, all of which poison the work environment. Your ultimate goal is to communicate a positive message, not to replace one negative message with another. You need to convince everyone that the success of each individual from now on depends on eliminating Negative Treatment in favor of a positive work environment. We are all stakeholders in the outcome.

6. **Create circumstances for positive interactions by helping people to get to know each other as individuals.** Here

your interactions with each person who reports to you can provide powerful motivation and an effective model for the behavior of others. In addition, you can encourage positive interactions with teamwork assignments, off-site events such as company-sponsored sports teams or gatherings, group bag lunches and any number of other activities you and your employees can imagine. The only limit is your creativity and the creativity of your team members. In addition, once you have focused on eliminating Negative Treatment and increasing positive interactions, you will probably find examples of new ideas and even leadership among those previously marginalized employees. In short, everybody wins.

It would be great if Negative Treatment could be eliminated just by becoming aware of it. But the obvious as well as unconscious and deeply ingrained tendencies toward exclusion take time and practice to master. We do not suggest that managers tolerate or acquiesce in such behavior during the learning process, but neither do we suggest that they focus on punishment or blame, although the responses to Negative Treatment must be open, swift and unambiguous. Once you have declared sexual harassment off limits, for example, you have to fire a salesman who continues to bother women colleagues even if he has great numbers. In the long run, however, a manager's powers of persuasion and influence will produce the enduring results. You have to convince your employees that Negative Treatment diminishes business results in order to motivate them to work toward the productivity promise.

QUALITY TREATMENT

The goal of the productivity promise means inclusive managers work not only to eliminate Negative Treatment but also to promote Quality Treatment, which we define as "constructive interactions with—or positive behavior consciously directed toward—an individual." Quality Treatment is really the answer to how managers and other influential members of an organization can "build capacity," thus significantly increasing the number of people who are performing at the high levels needed for continued business success.

The Quality Treatment Model in Figure 2.3 is the antidote to Negative Treatment.

In a work environment where Quality Treatment is the norm, managers and employees treat each other with respect and consideration. Such an environment is open and accepting of diversity in all its visible and invisible aspects. It is also characterized by teamwork and support between peers, as well as between managers and employees, as everyone works together to achieve common business goals. This type of environment doesn't just happen, but rather emerges out of a conscious decision on the part of managers at all levels to clearly define and model this behavior, and to hold themselves as well as employees accountable.

In addition, managers have to integrate Quality Treatment into every aspect of their supervisory roles. Thus, for managers, the required interactions and behavior with or toward all employees include:

- clear performance standards
- positive development opportunities
- ongoing feedback on progress
- appropriate emotional support.

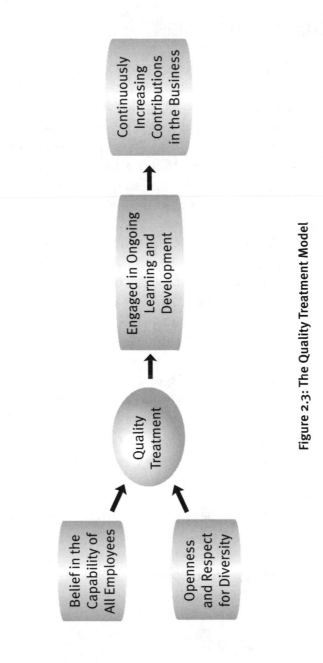

Figure 2.3: The Quality Treatment Model

Managers who practice Quality Treatment develop analytical and operational capabilities and self-confidence in every employee, with a focus on the organization's objectives. They set clear, high standards of performance for everyone and hold each person accountable for meeting that standard. The key idea is that performance is measured against the standard, not against the performance of other people. (For a more thorough discussion of setting standards, see Chapter 5.) Throughout the accountability process, managers provide encouragement, guidance and the firm belief that all employees can meet the standard. In this environment, each new capability inspires people to envision and pursue new challenges.

Quality Treatment inspires positive feelings, thoughts and behaviors. It actually builds confidence, which is the fuel for the capacity building model of development described in Chapter 1.

What is confidence, and why is it critical to workplace performance? Confidence at base means each person's belief that he or she can control, or can learn to control, performance outcomes. It is confidence that makes people willing to tackle new tasks. We already know that some people can keep their confidence up no matter what treatment they receive, so should we just assume it's not worth the effort to help those who can't do it on their own? We think that assumption leads to wasteful business decisions. Most of us have achieved whatever success we have because other people— family, teachers, friends, even casual acquaintances—supported us. The workplace is no different. All employees can and should choose to interact with people in ways deliberately designed to generate positive feelings, thoughts and behaviors. However, it remains the manager's job to *require* the kind of positive environment where the contributions of all are encouraged, supported and welcomed.

A major challenge in creating this positive environment for managers, already pressed from above for results, is patience, because new tasks are not necessarily mastered on the first try. Therefore Quality Treatment includes a willingness on the part of the manager to expect missteps as employees learn to take on stretch assignments. The managers' key strategy in this process is a pair of mutual obligations: the managers agree to give constructive feedback, and the employees agree to seek out and pay close attention to that feedback: "What do I need to do to get better? How must I change my approach? How can I ring the bell next time?" In this context, feedback is not a dreaded judgment about failure or limitations, it is a gift—the outline for an ongoing strategy of learning and improving. What was once "failure" is now information that points the way to improved performance.

Feedback is a fundamental component of the development process, perhaps the most critical one. Incorporating the information received from constructive feedback defines the next steps, and the pattern of continuous next steps leads to increased capacity and improved performance and the confidence to tackle more new tasks. It is the same upward spiral we have long witnessed for the talented few. But the process doesn't just work for a few. It works for almost all employees. We introduce the concept of constructive feedback here, but there is a more detailed discussion in Chapter 5.

Through feedback and other manifestations of Quality Treatment, we can maximize the likelihood of receiving the highest levels of performance from everybody. Here we are not talking about halfhearted attempts or just "getting by" with work performance. We are talking about employees who put forth "effective effort," which we define as tenacious engagement, a commitment to sticking with a difficult task until it is mastered, until the high standard is met. We see improved performance as a result of effective effort every day in cultures of development. The improved performance from employees who are fully engaged benefits the individual employees as well as the company overall. One mid-level manager we know, who worked for someone who assumed she had little to offer the company, summarized exactly why we continue to believe in the business value of inclusion and a culture of development. After numerous attempts at transfers, she finally landed in another department run by a manager who believed in her capabilities. After six months in her new job she shared her insights with us.

I used to be one of those people on the fringe, in danger of being totally disengaged from my job. I came to work only 30 to 40 percent ready to go, as opposed to a hundred percent every day, as I am now. Who your manager is makes such a huge difference in attitude and productivity. It's the difference between someone not performing up to par or just doing what's required and someone who's going above and beyond, meeting your wildest expectations. There are so many good people, with a lot of good skills and experience, but they just need that extra push to get them to the next level.

Are we being overly optimistic to believe that performance can be so easily and dramatically enhanced by Quality Treatment? We don't think so. We point to studies performed by Claude Steele, a social psychology professor at Stanford. He tested white, African-American and Asian-American male and female undergraduate students from across the country to determine the impact of what he calls "stereotype threat" on their ability to perform at a high level on standardized tests.

In controlled settings, test proctors either invoked or specifically discarded a common stereotype before a test. They then tested performance to see if it either declined or improved in direct response to the proctors' words. When, for example, women were told that a particular test was designed to measure their math ability and that most women do not perform very well on it, their performance suffered dramatically. Even white men fell prey to the stereotype threat: when told that Asian-Americans performed better on a certain math test, their performance declined, although not as dramatically as that of the women or blacks.

The reverse was also true. When, for example, African-Americans were told that the test did not measure ability but only psychological factors, they performed as well as whites on the same very challenging tests. In Professor Steele's conclusion, he did not focus on the fact that the stereotype threat is real and decreases people's ability to perform. Instead, he emphasized the positive aspect of the results—the ease with which the stereotype threat was neutralized. Merely stating that "ability" was not relevant to the test brought immediate and significant improvement in performance for groups whose ability had been continuously challenged by stereotypes.

What if workplaces adopted such a strategy? For example, what if conscious and unconscious signals about low expectations and false assumptions about lesser ability were replaced with a belief that everyone has potential for excellent performance? What if managers understood their job as identifying each person's interests or passions and current skills, nurturing and expanding them and then providing assignments that match them with company needs? What if, in addition, managers displayed genuine confidence in the abilities of all their employees? Professor Steele's studies suggest that the returns would come quickly because even subtle changes in treatment propel better performance—immediately.

In the next chapter, Chapter 3, we take a closer look at the skills managers need to develop in order to provide Quality Treatment to all employees. We will focus on one key component of Quality Treatment—positioning employees so that they have access to the challenging assignments and other opportunities that will enable them to continuously develop and augment their contributions to the business. In Chapter 5, we detail what human resources leaders can do to support managers in these efforts and to support Quality Treatment and a culture of development throughout the organization.

CHAPTER THREE

Managing Inclusion

Positioning All Employees for Success

*We rely on a knowledge-powered workforce, and there's
a direct correlation between how managers treat them
(employees) and how they perform. So we're focused
on educating the managers—those who "own" the
environment and touch the lives of each worker.*

Carlton Yearwood
Chief Diversity Officer
Waste Management, Inc.

We know from experience that an inclusive culture of development succeeds or fails in the one-on-one relationships between
managers and their employees, played out in hundreds of interactions every day. With their direct involvement in the work of each
employee, from assignments, supervision, guidance, motivation

and support, to performance review, managers are the only people in a position to unlock the potential of each employee. The best managers have the capacity to mold, coach, coax, build and inspire the best performance possible. If there is going to be an inclusive culture, they are the ones who will build it.

As a manager, you may ask, "How can I, in my small circle of influence, possibly be very important to my company's business results?" The truth is that in an economy where products and services are based on knowledge, the contribution of each person matters. Every employee is in a position to keep customers enthusiastic about services and products—each one may be a customer's only contact with a company. It is line managers who inspire the continuing contributions of their employees day in and day out. Your work as a manager is critical to the culture of development.

What are the skills that make a great manager? Think back to the best teacher or coach you had in school, and how he or she was able to inspire you to try harder and perform better than you ever imagined you could. That's pretty much the same thing we're suggesting you do in managing your employees. In our workshops, we ask participants to describe the best boss they ever had. The responses typically include variations of the following:

Trusted me with important work.

Helped me learn from my mistakes.

Gave me opportunities to learn and grow.

Really wanted me to succeed.

Most companies promote people to managerial positions based on their technical skills or their outstanding performance in a specific area important to the company's business objectives. But managing people is very different from completing a work project, your only responsibility before becoming a manager. Does the promotion mean people automatically know how to manage? Are good managers born that way—is it a case of "some have it and some don't?" (And didn't we discuss that same thing about a select few employees earlier?) Is management an innate skill, something that comes naturally? We find few come to management positions knowing how to manage, even though most companies operate as if they do. One of our clients described the quandary.

> *Sure I was happy to be promoted. But the only training I got when I started was how to fill out the annual performance evaluation. For two years I've been learning as I go along, reading books and all. But some real training at the front end would have made a big difference.*

Companies in general provide little or no training for those who take on this critical business role. When clients ask us for help, we offer Managing Inclusion, Novations's copyrighted training for managers. This chapter describes that training in detail.

Just as with other types of talent, managerial skills are learned through a process of development, what you need to know to be able to inspire the best performance in all your employees. Some might question why managers should bother to learn these new skills. What's in it for them? Thanks to downsizing and outsourcing, most managers are already overwhelmed with additional work. We understand that it can be difficult to step back and think of the long-term benefits in the midst of daily crisis management, but we ask managers to consider the long-term benefits of taking such actions.

We can easily identify several compelling arguments.

1. Do you have a few "go-to" people, the ones you turn to for most of your key assignments? Wouldn't your life be easier if you had more "go-to" people? With so few of them, what will you do if one of them leaves, say, for a different job in your company or another company, or is absent for a long period because of illness? A culture of development promises relief from these stresses. Yes, it takes time that is difficult to find in the present. But we ask you to keep your eye on the future—both your future and the future of your organization. With more employees realizing their potential and performing at their peak, you can expect to meet your business goals more effectively, and chances are that your own career will also benefit as a result.

2. There are less tangible rewards, for example, the satisfaction that comes from seeing your efforts lead to new achievement by others. A former Home Depot board member who has been personally involved in that process many times explains the satisfaction:

    The experience and confidence you give to people on a team is just unbelievable. And they can go off and do it themselves and feel proud for a long, long time. That's pretty special . . . It goes beyond the project, even beyond the workplace.

3. And there is the personal sense of accomplishment that comes from engaging in your own process of development, your new awareness of the expanding role you play in the business success of your company. You bring value that goes beyond your own contributions, by working through others to inspire their greater contributions.

CONTINUOUS IMPROVEMENT

Success in business is measured by a company's ability to deliver products and services that customers want. This may seem too obvious to bother stating, but it is the starting point for understanding why your role as a manager has a direct impact on your company's bottom line. To meet the competitive challenges of today's fast-paced global marketplace, a company's products and services must continuously improve. Products and services that are satisfactory, or even outstanding, today will not be good enough tomorrow. Now that products and services are increasingly knowledge-based at companies in the West and in more and more parts of Asia, the only way to maintain a competitive edge is to have a workforce where every employee contributes his or her best to the process of continuous improvement. That's the only way to be prepared for tomorrow's challenges.

LEARNING LOOPS

How do products and services get improved? Think about it. All new ideas are the result of human learning. That means all employees must learn everything possible about how the company's products and services presently operate or function, including their problems and deficiencies. It means learning what works for customers and clients and what doesn't, and then having the courage and innovative skill to envision something better and make it happen. It should be pretty obvious that we are not talking about learning that leads to one improvement, because one improvement in a product, process or service is not enough. One improvement is merely the platform for additional learning and the next round of improvements. Business needs new ideas constantly, so we are talking about a process of continuous learning that naturally leads to continuous improvements.

We call the mutually reinforcing relationship between continuous learning and continuous improvement a "Learning Loop" (see Figure 3.1). To remain competitive, organizations need every possible employee engaged in Learning Loops focused on the business's key products and services. Managers play an essential role in this process by encouraging employees to stretch themselves and then making it safe for them to continue engaging in Learning Loops.

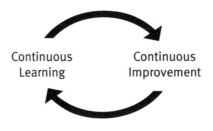

Figure 3.1: The Learning Loop

Employees involved in Learning Loops are valuable to the company in any job, at any level in the organization, and at any point in their career. A building maintenance person who devises a new process for cleaning the HVAC systems, the file clerk who designs a more user-friendly filing system, or the sales rep who recognizes a new client need even before the client does, are all examples of the bottom-line value each employee can bring to the company by engaging in Learning Loops—continuous learning and continuous improvements.

To better understand this dynamic, envision Learning Loops as three-dimensional, with both employees and products spiraling upward. There is no end to the possibilities. Rather than going around in circles, this is an upward spiral of improving skills, knowledge and confidence (see Figure 3.2).

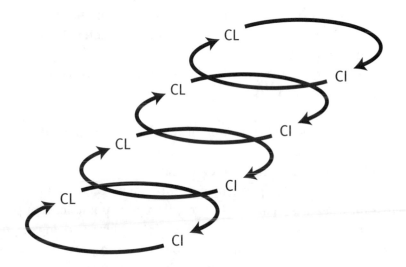

Figure 3.2: The 3-D Learning Loop

Learning Loops are two-way value propositions, benefiting both the company and the employees engaged in them. Every time employees successfully master new job-related skills, every time they offer new ideas for improving products and services, they improve themselves and increase their personal job satisfaction. More important, they are going to enjoy that feeling of success and want to take on more challenges. When employees engage in Learning Loops on behalf of a company's products and services, constantly stretching their capabilities and contributing to the company's business objectives, they typically exhibit the following characteristics:

- They apply their intellect and effort to their work.
- They understand the company's business objectives and how their work contributes to those objectives.
- They focus on understanding and meeting the needs of customers and clients, throughout the company and in the broader marketplace.
- They are constantly on the alert to find ways to reduce costs and increase profits.

Isn't this a good description of your "go to" people—the employees everyone wants? Their success is based on an attitude or a mindset tenaciously engaged every day in improving individual, group and company performance. Most managers would agree that they need as many of these employees as possible. Companies that successfully encourage all their employees to engage in Learning Loops—to learn continuously and improve continuously—will easily be more competitive than companies who do not.

Yet when we ask managers what percentage of their employees are actively engaged in Learning Loops relevant to the business, we regularly hear very small numbers. There is always a range, usually between 5 per cent and 30 per cent, but most managers come down in the range of 15 per cent to 20 per cent. That means that fully 80 per cent of the workforce is not engaged in efforts to improve the bottom line. What can managers do about this waste of potential? To us at Novations the answer is obvious. They can create positions for learning and development for all their people, while providing the necessary support for success.

CREATING "POSITION"

When we compare the people who are engaged in a process of continuous learning and development with the many others who seldom, if ever, approach that level of contribution to the business, we find two complementary factors operating. We call them "Position" and "Disposition."

It is important to emphasize that by "Position" we do *not* mean a job title or a particular level in the organization's hierarchy. Instead, we are referring to the *characteristics* of a specific assignment given to an employee and the accompanying support he or she receives. As we discussed in Chapter 2, the stretch assignments and accompanying support are essential parts of the Quality Treatment that inclusive managers provide to their employees.

An assignment has positive "Position" if it:

- represents a platform for learning,
- stimulates the development of analytical, operational and team-related skills, and
- includes managerial support and encouragement for the new effort, including constructive, honest and open feedback about performance, both positive and negative.

A senior executive, for example, who has been "put out to pasture" and therefore receives no challenging assignments, does not have positive Position. But an up-and-coming individual contributor who is assigned to work on a marketing team designing the campaign for a new product does. One conclusion that is immediately clear is that managers have a direct impact on Position because they dispense the work assignments.

It should come as no surprise that in many organizations the same few people receive a disproportionately large percentage of positive Positions. One senior vice-president of HR we work with gave an example of what his company found when they began to analyze the impact of the assignment process on their employees who were women and people of color:

> When one African-American woman kept getting labeled "She's not strategic," I finally asked her manager, "What does that mean? Has she ever had a job that required her to be strategic? How does one get to be strategic, if you've only had jobs that required you to be task oriented? Let's put her in the job. Let's give her some support, some guidance. That's the way it happened for me, and probably you as well." So she got the chance to start exercising her strategic muscle in a relatively low-risk and supportive environment, and she did fine. Those are the discoveries we're starting to make. That's the way to harness development energy.

That same vice-president goes on to question the unconscious thinking that often excludes people from those stretch assignments, and thus from any real success:

Why is it that we're afraid to take a risk with her, and we're not afraid with a white guy?" It's that unconscious risk analysis that has to be examined. Once managers realize they are making assignments based on subjective and unexamined assumptions, they are more apt to be open to developing the potential of all their employees.

As a manager, you may think that your job is complete when you dispense key assignments to a broader number of employees, but you would be wrong. Your work is just beginning. People with their first stretch assignment need your attention and your guidance.

- Have you provided the right level of challenge for a particular person?
- Do you know that person well enough to know if the leap is too small to require developing new skills or too great to achieve success?

You need to be prepared to monitor progress and to provide guidance if necessary or appropriate. Then you need to provide constructive, honest and open feedback.

- What worked well?
- Why?
- What needs improvement?
- How?

This includes treating honest mistakes as learning opportunities.

Supplying ongoing feedback is critical if the process of growth and development is to continue. A manager's feedback should always have the goal of urging employees to move from the role of independent contributor to that of contributing through others. Companies need a critical mass of employees who can inspire confidence in other people, who can effectively encourage others to take on risk and improve their skills. Given the opportunity, support and encouragement to stretch, many more people will rise to the occasion. Doesn't that seem like a better strategy for long-term success than assuming most employees have little to offer and concentrating all on a select few?

AFFECTING "DISPOSITION"

Up to now we've been talking about the manager's role in creating Position for all employees, that is, supporting their learning and development. But this is only half of the equation, since employees have the responsibility to respond appropriately. "Disposition" can be viewed as the flip side of the "Position" coin, focusing on an individual's response to "Position," either positive or negative. We define Disposition as:

- the degree to which an employee demonstrates the confidence, determination and commitment
- necessary to take advantage of all available opportunities for learning and leadership, and
- to expand the range of his or her skills and capabilities.

It might seem that Disposition is entirely up to each individual employee, and there is some truth to that conclusion. But, as it turns out, managers can and often do have an impact on

Disposition as well, both positive and negative. There is a critical link between treatment and performance.

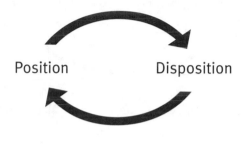

Figure 3.3: Position/Disposition Model

In our training with managers around the globe, we often ask them for examples of times they were not Positioned well and how this negative Position affected their Disposition. When people are treated poorly or are simply ignored and not given opportunities to learn, their confidence and motivation are undermined. They develop negative Disposition, and managers looking at those people understandably feel justified in denying them challenging assignments and support. Negative Disposition makes it far less likely that someone will ever receive learning opportunities and support—in short, positive Position.

Think back to a time when you were excluded, say, from an assignment you really wanted. How did it make you feel? Did your commitment level drop? Did you complain? Did you apply yourself so you got the next best assignment? Most people take such experiences in stride and get themselves back in the game. But what if your experience was to be criticized and excluded most of the time? Wouldn't it be harder each time to re-commit yourself?

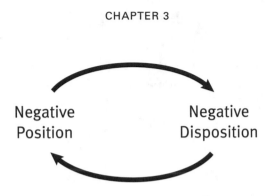

Figure 3.4: Negative Position/Negative Disposition Model

People who are denied good Position can quite reasonably feel justified in their lack of commitment to the work. This is not true in all situations, but it is true of many. When people are treated poorly or are simply ignored and not given opportunities to learn, their confidence and motivation are undermined. They develop negative Disposition, and managers looking at those people understandably feel justified in denying them challenging assignments and support. Negative Disposition makes it far less likely that someone will ever receive learning opportunities and support—positive Position.

Over time, a chronic negative Disposition can develop as a result of years of being excluded, harshly criticized or otherwise treated negatively. Here are some typical manifestations when there's been a pattern of ongoing negative Position.

1. **Unproductive anger**, either displayed—by overreacting to minor issues, for example—or hidden, sometimes behind a sullen façade.

    It can be very difficult for employees to get beyond that anger, especially if it is associated with feeling victimized— "How could they have denied me a promotion all these years when I helped train people who are vice-presidents now?" People coming from that very emotional place can't usually articulate their feelings openly, even when an empathetic manager begins asking them. It takes time to trust and to adjust to that positive change in the work environment.

2. **Simply holding back.** One manager described his frustration with many of his colleagues' refusal to get involved.

   There are so many employees who say they want to move up, but when you reach out to them—take a look at this job opportunity—you'll see that hesitation. You'll see that fear about coming out of their comfort zone, that place where they finally feel comfortable.

3. **Dragging down their colleagues.** One manager described how understanding the cause of this "crabs in the barrel" behavior helped her respond to it more effectively.

   When I see employees pulling other employees down, I don't like it. But when you understand where it comes from, you have another level of patience and understanding. Then you can do something about getting them out of that destructive behavior.

It's difficult to erase the effects of years of neglect, or even one really negative work experience, overnight. Therefore the challenge inclusive managers face is how to help these employees take advantage of new opportunities in spite of what they may have experienced in the past. A chief diversity officer describes her own realization:

It takes so much positive reinforcement to unlearn so much negative reinforcement. But once I understood that, I've been able to keep going, even when it seems like I'm not making progress.

HOW MANAGERS REVERSE NEGATIVE DISPOSITION

Because any negative Disposition harms business performance, managers need to find strategies first to neutralize it and then transform it. Managers in our training programs again point the way for some of the critical elements in providing positive Position as a way of reversing and building positive Disposition. After we've asked them about their examples when they were not in a good Position, we ask them what actions on the part of their managers would have made a difference in their situations.

The most important action managers can take to influence the Disposition of employees is to Position them for learning, development and success. This includes providing the support and trust that are part of Position. Once managers have a clear understanding of the link between treatment and performance, they will understand their ability to influence behavior. The simple first step is to refocus your assignment process to reflect your new awareness. This kind of change is totally in the hands of individual managers; there is no need for a new corporate policy, no need for approval from a manager's manager. And the results will speak for themselves.

Figure 3.5: Positive Position/Positive Disposition Model

Some people will respond very quickly. All they need is a slight push in the right direction. When confidence is more deeply marred, the change process will be slower. There, you need both an open mind and perseverance. Here are some specific steps managers can take:

1. **Explore the symptoms in a non-judgmental way**, observing your employees' behavior through a new lens, to find the root causes, paying attention to those who may be giving Negative Treatment as well as those that may be receiving it. How do they relate to you? To each other? Do you see anger? Do you see holding back, hesitance or refusal to get involved? Do you see malicious compliance, following instructions to the letter but not to the spirit? Do you see boredom? Frequent late arrival at work? Missed deadlines? Sloppy work? Excuses, such as blaming others?

2. **Watch what others do to them.** Is work being sabotaged? Do you find unkind jokes? Teasing and criticism, behind the back or to someone's face? You will often find surprising circumstances and situations behind these unproductive

outward behaviors. What new insights can you draw from the specifics you find in your department?

3. **Review their work history through this same lens of curiosity, not judgment.** Include their performance with you and before you knew them. What are their strengths and challenges? How would you plan constructive feedback to them if you have not done so in the past? What are their interests? What are the topics that engage them? Do you see how the evidence of Negative Treatment has affected their performance? What can you do differently?

4. **Develop strategies to begin to address the Negative Treatment and its negative consequences.** Depending on your relationships and the depth of the problems, you might decide to call them into your office for a straightforward discussion. Being understood is usually a key ingredient in being able to overcome Negative Disposition. In some cases you might decide it's better to be less direct, using, for example, a work assignment as the process for opening a dialogue. You can undoubtedly devise many other workable strategies, based on your new knowledge of the individual.

5. **In all cases, agree on a standard of appropriate behavior for the future**, perhaps even a timetable. You will want to support the process of change, especially by keeping in touch with appropriate feedback. As one diversity director explained it,

    When you understand where the other person is coming from, you can create a common agenda. That's been my strategy. I tell them, "You don't have to put your tail

*between your legs and think, 'Woe is me, I fell down."
Just get up and say, 'Okay, that didn't work,' and make
some adjustments."*

6. **Tolerate honest mistakes and use them as learning opportunities**. Reinforce that failure and difficulty are information about how to improve, not a condemnation of the ability or worth of the individual. Clarify the new standards, if necessary. Help them to understand the feedback about what they need to do differently. Continue to coach and direct their efforts to promote learning and expanding independence.

7. **Refuse to accept low performance or to give up in frustration**. Few of these learned behaviors will change overnight. Consistent support and encouragement will eventually yield better results from almost everyone. Keep engineering the next incremental challenge that will build confidence and support learning.

    The few who really cannot respond can be placed elsewhere if there is an indication that another department or different work team might better suit their interests or skills. You may also need to counsel the individual to seek a different opportunity outside the company where they are more likely to be successful. In all those cases, keep the focus on what it takes to ensure that the individual can put forth effective effort, not on his or her presumed limitations. In this way, the experience, even if difficult, can be confidence building—or at the very least, not confidence destroying.

MANAGING INCLUSION FOR ALL YOUR EMPLOYEES

We've discussed the need for continuous learning and continuous improvement on the part of all employees in order to achieve business success, along with the critical role that managers play in that process. The manager's role involves managing both Position and Disposition so that employees will have the commitment and determination to take advantage of new opportunities. Now we are ready to outline a strategy to build on these ideas and concepts so that managers can use them to launch an inclusive process of development with their employees. We've divided this strategy into two parts—short-term (or "jump-start") and ongoing or long-term.

Short-Term "Jump-Start"

There are many steps that you, as a manager, can take immediately to start promoting positive Position among those who report to you. These are steps you can just decide to take, without any approval from above.

1. **Conduct a quick audit of your present work distribution.**

   Do you find that the most interesting, challenging and important assignments always go to the same "usual suspects," the "go-to" people, the small number of people you feel are most reliable?

2. **Think about broadening the work distribution.**

   A good place to start is by enhancing the Position of one or two people who have not received challenging assignments in the past. You can do that immediately by restructuring existing assignments to make them more challenging and relevant to business objectives. For example, one sales manager had her experienced sales reps serve as coaches for new reps and factored that into their bonuses. As a result, the gearing-up time for new reps was significantly reduced.

Then, as new projects or assignments reach your desk, you can distribute them beyond the usual suspects. You can test the waters and increase the level of challenge for each employee as you deem appropriate.

3. **Support your people.**

Make sure you give special attention to the people who are dealing with their first challenging assignments. Consult with them on the nature of the job, provide regular feedback and make it clear that they can come to you with questions, that your door is truly open for ongoing support. The real object of a process of development is to engineer success, not just to confer better assignments.

Longer-Term Strategy

These steps work in tandem with the short-term steps, but, because many of them have implications beyond your own department, you may need approval from or consultation with, say, human resources. They will almost all require more planning, investigation and preparation on your part.

1. **Identify the same high standard of expected performance for every employee, and express the belief that each one is capable of meeting it.**

If your company is like most companies and has not pre-pared and distributed high-quality behavioral competencies, you may have to start the process yourself, so you can set ex-pectations and document progress for each employee. The high standard of excellence for everyone must be the same, but it will take a lot of effort on your part to get everyone to the same starting point.

For work already in progress, or for those employees you already have a working relationship with, an informal col-laborative process will probably prove to be the best strategy, even though it will take more time initially. You can start the conversation with them by taking the job description and, if you have not already done so as a part of the annual review process, drawing up specific performance requirements for each work assignment. For your other employees, the process will be the same, but it will take longer. You will have to build the trusting work relationship from both sides.

Throughout this process, you need to make sure that your standards are as objective as possible. That means focusing on desired results and outcomes in a work as-signment rather than on each step to reach those results. People have different work styles, as well as thought and analysis patterns; many different paths lead to the desired result. Managers who are open to this reality have learned that these differences often allow employees to uncover new approaches and improvements. If your standards restrict their behavior purely for subjective reasons, not only do you close off avenues of inquiry and discovery beyond your own perspective, you also stifle the confidence that comes from mastering a task on one's own. That confidence is the key element in a culture of development; it is what inspires people to engage in Learning Loops.

We have found that you need to be explicit about your belief that everyone can hit the same high standard. You cannot assume that oblique or casual references will resonate the same way with everyone. We point specifically to the need to make sure that every woman, person of color and other diverse group member clearly understands the performance expectations and believes that you believe in their capacity to achieve at that level. Many of them come in expecting you to have little confidence in their ability, so your honest, open and firm approach can begin to dispel their concerns that you won't support their development. Belief in the potential of everyone is not just a phrase; it needs to be a conscious part of your interactions with each of your employees.

It may be difficult to get past the negative Dispositions of some of your employees and focus on their hidden capabilities. You can think of it as a leap of faith, just to get yourself going. But if you really examine your own past experience, it's no more a leap of faith to start with high expectations than it is to start with low expectations—consciously or unconsciously. Facing low expectations, most people will live down to them. A positive belief, on the other hand, often brings surprising results. We know of one West Coast telephone company office in a poor neighborhood that had experienced the lowest customer satisfaction results in the company for years. A new manager arrived with a positive set of expectations for her employees along with the willingness to support them. In one year their customer satisfaction results were the second best in the company. As one employee described it,

At first we didn't trust her—thought she was just trying to make us do more work. But after a while most of us saw

she was serious about helping us get better. For the first
time in ten years I began feeling proud about my work.

This is not an isolated example; these strategies work. You
can probably think of a few times in your career when you
overlooked someone who was in fact highly motivated, capable and deeply committed to making a contribution. All that
person needed was your expectation and conscious display
of support to begin tapping into his or her own potential. We
acknowledge that there will be some employees who require
more effort than others. However, we believe absolutely—and
our experience confirms our belief—that in almost all cases
slower learning is the result of lower confidence, not lower
ability. Your challenge as a manager is to find an approach
that works. Great managers inspire great results, and many of
those results are surprises.

2. **Frame Positions in terms of their contribution to the busi-
    ness objectives**, and build assignments for all your employees
    that will encourage continuous development of their analyti-
    cal and operational skills.

    Restructuring job assignments and linking each one to
    business goals is a relatively easy and objective process. Ar-
    riving at the right level of challenge for each employee, how-
    ever, requires more insight and a more complex equation for
    decision-making. Setting high expectations rather than low
    ones does not mean that you simply express your belief and
    then your job is done. Your challenge is to *develop* potential,
    not merely declare it. Building capacity and confidence takes
    time, and there are few shortcuts.

In designing a work assignment, the best place to start is with information about the employee, drawn from your knowledge of his or her prior experience, along with your own interactions and observations. Then you can begin to focus on what will be challenging for that person at this time. You need to find the point where an assignment asks a particular employee to take a risk, but is also likely to bring success—given committed, strategic effort. One that poses too great a stretch can result in less than excellent performance or even failure—thus undermining whatever confidence the employee does have.

On the other hand, if there is no challenge and no risk-taking, there is little to be gained. And people recognize a manager who underestimates their capability.

My boss would talk to me like I was a cream puff. He only gave me simple little boring assignments, when I was looking for something I could really sink my teeth into. I kind of felt he thought I could only go so far, maybe that I'd already gone farther than I should have to begin with.

You can manage this development process by getting to know your employees. What is their work history? What are their career interests? What issues fire their imaginations? You can gather this information through conversations, shared experiences and reports from others who have worked with them. What opportunities do you find when you look closely at their work products, factoring in all your new information? Then use the individual information and your real relationships as the basis for engineering an appropriate stretch work assignment. It is a collaborative process, with no set rules, but based on individual learning styles and work styles. Confidence—and therefore development—comes from a conscious process of incremental stretches: taking on appropriate risks, succeeding, making mistakes and learning from them, and then using the new platform to set more ambitious goals. Your job is to manage that process. You want your people to be improving, not simply proving over and over that they can do something they have already done before.

3. **Reinforce the efforts of your employees by encouraging and rewarding their learning.**

Even after you have redistributed your assignments, your job is not done. You still need to pay attention to the work process, to check on progress as well as confidence level, and to provide guidance and encouragement as necessary. In this way you can be ready either to suggest additional challenges or slow down the process, whichever is appropriate.

With stretch assignments, your nonjudgmental support along the way can mean the difference between success and failure. In addition to reaching out, you also need to be truly open to requests for guidance from your employees. Some employees may find it easy to demand support, but others will not even know to ask for it, let alone how to approach a boss.

I never asked for any help because I was raised to believe we had to do things on our own. That was certainly the way it was in school, and no one told me it was different at work. I didn't know that others were asking for and getting help.

Your employees should all understand that your door is literally and figuratively open, that they can turn to you without fear you will be annoyed or hold their questions against them. This openness is a key factor in encouraging learning and appropriate risk-taking in those who report to you.

Your reinforcement is needed when employees take a risk, even a carefully calculated risk, because of course, failure is always a possibility. No one succeeds every time. Some failure, as every successful person knows, is inevitable, but it is never proof of lesser ability. Failure, in fact, is simply data telling you that you have to improve in the future, so that you can say to yourself: "Now I know what will not work, and I can use that experience to design a new strategy that will be successful." When the inevitable failures happen, your response as a manager is crucial. Will the employee fear being fired or taking risks in the future, or will he or she come back with renewed vigor? Remember the story of Tom Watson, the founder of IBM, from Chapter 1, and make it clear that mistakes are okay, so long as they lead to improved direction. Your job is to inspire more effective effort and to stave off diminished confidence, because the real value of your employees is based on their willingness to engage in Continuous Improvement aligned with business objectives.

4. **Provide constructive, honest and open feedback on a regular basis,** so strategies for learning and improving are continuously refined and serve as platforms for the next cycle in the Learning Loop.

    Why is providing feedback such a persistent stumbling block for most managers? First, most of us think of feedback as bad news—rather than as a means to learning. And it is as

uncomfortable to deliver bad news as it is to receive it. Even
though it is the manager's job to initiate feedback, not surprisingly, many seek every excuse to avoid doing so. As one
HR executive put it,

I describe feedback to my colleagues as castor oil. We all
hate it, but we do it anyway because we know it's good
for us. That's the deal.

He added, however, that those who have gotten used to
the process swear by it, especially those on the receiving end.

It's interesting to me that most successful people, as
much as they hate hearing feedback, they're eager to
receive it. "Just tell me what I'm doing wrong." They're
so driven to do better that they're willing to put up with
the pain of listening to almost anything if they believe it's
going to help make them better. And those people make
their managers understand feedback is doing folks a real
service.

Another problem with feedback is the amount of time
it takes to do the job right. Here's how one HR executive explained the dilemma.

A lot of managers don't want to have these discussions
because what should have taken a half hour turns into
a three-hour conversation, and some people just aren't
going to listen to what you say anyway. If everything's
not fine, I'm not helping you or the organization by telling

you that it is. He's going to argue with you, but you have to say, "If you want to kid yourself and have me say that everything's rosy, fine, I'll do it. But you're not going to grow professionally, and you're not going to understand why you don't get those promotions."

It's the easiest thing in the world for a manager to say, "Everything's fine."

It's a quick discussion, and everybody goes away happy. But if you're serious about a culture of development, no one should accept the argument that there is not enough time. The time you spend giving effective feedback is well worth the effort when you think about the time, effort and financial resources wasted when employees who have not received timely feedback continue to make unnecessary mistakes and are not inspired to work up to their potential.

5. **Be consciously aware of the special challenges involved in providing effective feedback to employees who are different from you**, and make a special effort to overcome those challenges.

An aspect that merits special attention in the universally difficult issue of feedback is the challenge of giving feedback to someone different from oneself, whether it's a difference in work style, personality, race, gender, sexual orientation, age, physical ability, or ethnic or cultural origin. Some managers are genuinely afraid of saying the "wrong thing" and provoking formal or informal charges of discrimination. Even a champion of diversity, a white man who is head of North American sales for a consumer company, voices that common and understandable concern.

It's hard enough for a lot of people to sit across the desk talking to another white male. It's not easy to tell anybody he or she's not performing well. But it's a more difficult conversation when you're looking across the desk at an African-American man or woman. I think there are a lot of people who are afraid of saying the wrong thing. They're thinking through every word. Which word will be the one that's going to be wrong? Which word will be taken out of context and used against me?

Behind all business success is calculated risk. So if you as a manager have created an inclusive environment, then your open and honest, constructive feedback is more likely to produce improved performance than a grievance. Almost all employees want to make valuable contributions to their companies, and they know the price they pay in their careers when they aren't able to do so. One client described how difficult it was for her to accept simply being passed along.

I think because I am an African-American female, many people danced around honest and open feedback. Not to say I ran amok throughout my career, but people were not comfortable saying a lot of things to me. Were they afraid I would sue the company? I don't know. But they said nothing, and I just continued to get moved through the system. You're not being the person you could be, because you're not getting that open and honest feedback from anyone.

It will always be true that some people, regardless of their background, do not handle criticism, even constructive criticism, well. But most people know that they need guidance, especially when working on something new and challenging. The concerns of managers are real, but the company's interest is not protected if a manager sidesteps giving the necessary feedback. Both the employees and the company lose out when managers fail to perform a key part of the managerial job.

GOOD TO GREAT

As we have seen throughout this chapter, being a great manager means engaging in your own Learning Loops—continuously learning and continuously improving. At first it will be difficult and take a great deal of time, especially since mid-level downsizing has often left managers with responsibility for too many employees and even their own tasks and assignments, beyond the work of others they must supervise. Continuous learning does get easier with practice, and it promises meaningful rewards for you as well as your company. Being a great manager will make your job more satisfying, and you will enjoy coming to work even more. And as a great manager, the value you bring to your company will multiply.

Having said this, we realize that managers, like all employees, are more willing to examine their assumptions and try out new behaviors when they understand the importance of these actions to the business and, more important, when they see their leaders modeling these behaviors. In Chapter 4 we focus on the special roles that senior leaders play in building and sustaining an inclusive culture of development.

CHAPTER FOUR

Strategic Leadership
The Sine Qua Non of Change

Inclusion—people development—has to be incorporated into every business initiative. If you wanted to roll out a new advertising plan, a new marketing plan, a change in the way your assembly line functions, you'd roll certain key things throughout the company, to make sure they're consistent with your values, your market objectives. Why would inclusion be any different?

> Faye Wilson
> Member of the Board (ret.)
> The Home Depot, Inc.

Based on our thirty years of consulting, we know that many organizations have spent considerable time and money on inclusion and other initiatives designed to develop a broader range of employees—special leadership training, mentoring, recruiting, internships, scholarships, work with community organizations, and the list goes on. Despite these efforts, data indicate that in many organizations all but a few are not advancing beyond the middle levels and are unhappy with their performance ratings, work assignments and future prospects. As a result, too many employees are choosing not to engage fully with their work or they are voting with their feet, leaving to find greater satisfaction in more welcoming environments. We can't give up, so what more can or should be done?

We firmly believe that progress toward greater inclusion and cultures of development have been made and will continue to be made around the world. However, leveraging that truth and its potential for economic growth are evolving processes, and there will be both successes and setbacks.

Although there should be no question about the ultimate goal, we still face many open issues about how to move from where most organizations are today to an inclusive culture of development. No matter what the open issues, the challenges or the individual culture of an organization, we find one factor in success that does not vary: senior leaders, especially the CEO, must view inclusion and development as strategic business imperatives, commit to achieving them, incorporate them into every aspect of business strategy and demand accountability at every level in the organization.

THE ROLE OF LEADERS IN SUSTAINABLE CULTURE CHANGE

We begin by examining the process of behavioral change, because changing an organization's culture requires that the behaviors—and ultimately the values—of individual members change. This process follows a predictable model of ever-deepening commitment on the part of individuals that was first developed by Harvard social psychologist Herbert C. Kelman in the 1960s and introduced to a broader audience in his book with colleague V. Lee Hamilton in 1989, *Crimes of Obedience*. Novations founder Jeff Howard applied the model to building an inclusive corporate culture.

Change is hard-won, because cultural norms and resulting behaviors are deeply embedded in any individual's psyche. The first level of behavior change is *compliance*, where individuals obey a command from senior leaders in order to receive a reward or avoid a punishment. Here, the changed behavior on the part of each individual is relatively easy to achieve, but it lasts only as long as an authority figure is within hearing distance.

The second and deeper level is *identification*, where individuals accept the leader's commitment as the model for their own behavior. Here, individuals understand that the behavior is required in order to be valued in the organization. Because they want to be so valued, they begin to police their own behavior. However, in today's world, where mergers, restructuring and change of leadership are the norm, there is no guarantee that committed leaders will remain at the helm of any organization. Will new leaders espouse the same values, for example, inclusion and a culture of development? It is not unusual for new leadership to coincide with loss of momentum on any number of initiatives. Unfortunately, while forward progress on behavior change moves at a snail's pace, reversion to the original behavior point happens in a flash. When identification is the reason for behavior change, if the leader who has been actively committed leaves and momentum slows, people's behavior is most likely to revert to the previous norm.

To ensure that inclusion-related values and practices remain despite a change in leadership, people must first reach the deepest level of commitment—*internalization*. At this level, inclusive behavior is no longer either grudging or modeled; it is a statement about an individual's own values. People who have internalized the values become independent agents working to keep the behavior of others on track.

The critical role of strategic leadership is apparent at every level of the process to change behavior. In compliance, leadership is the source of the rewards and the punishments, and behavior will follow their rules. In identification, employees are modeling the behavior and the tone of leadership they admire. After an extended period of compliance and identification, when employees from their own experience have learned that inclusion and a culture of development is better for them and for the business, comes internalization. Employees no longer need rewards, punishment or role models; they have adopted inclusion and development as their own values. To reach the point of internalization requires a long commitment on the part of leadership, so it is not surprising that progress is slow. Yet many of the senior leaders we consult with are frustrated. We hear statements similar to this one frequently:

I believe in inclusion. I know it's the right thing to do.
I personally launched our Diversity Council and spent

about one-third of my annual address emphasizing how important inclusion and development are for our business. But how can I convince others in the organization that I'm really serious?

Although most companies are still at the compliance or identification levels, and the journey ahead will not be quick or easy, some employees are impatient. Leaders who are frustrated, therefore, have reason to be concerned, for the many inclusion assessments we have conducted show how difficult it is to dispel suspicions that the leader's message is merely talk. When asked what they would need to see to believe their leaders are truly committed to inclusion, the answers almost always focus on visible and active involvement, on modeling inclusion and on holding other managers accountable for inclusive behavior. Here are some typical statements.

Our VP talks about respecting and including everyone, but he passes me every day and never has time to stop and say hi.

Managers around here are only evaluated on meeting their production goals. They are never held accountable for how they treat us.

If our CEO were really committed, he would take the time to understand what's really going on in this company—why only some people get ahead—and then do something about it. Right now I don't think he has a clue.

Yeah, we have Diversity and Inclusion Councils, but there's no link between them and anyone on the 16th floor. And their recommendations never get acted on. The Councils are just something nice that the CEO can talk about and put on our Web site.

There is one manager everyone knows has problems with women, but his numbers are good, so nothing happens to him.

They talk about "in the pipeline," but no one ever comes out the other end.

We've got a woman on our board, but she is not on the compensation or nominations committee. We all know it's just a token.

UNDERSTAND THE BUSINESS CASE

So what advice do we give these well-meaning and frustrated leaders? First, in order to be truly authentic when verbalizing the importance of inclusion and development, leaders need to "do their homework"—to fully understand the business case as it applies to their industry and organization. This book is devoted to making that case: inclusion and a culture of development, where all employees are encouraged to maximize their potential, will result in a company maximizing its productivity. In a service economy, where the contribution of each employee is critical to success, the ability of a company to inspire this process of continuous learning and continuous improvement in every employee will define its competitive advantage.

Although all of our experience convinces us that inclusion and a culture of development can and will improve the productivity of every company around the world, it is U.S. companies that have the most experience working toward those twin goals. Therefore, we look for a moment at two major trends which will converge on corporate America over the next decade or so. Together they signal urgency in establishing an inclusive culture of development as well as a unique opportunity for transformational corporate change. The first is the wave of CEOs and other senior leaders—members of the baby-boom generation, those born following the end of World War II—who are retiring and will continue to retire. The second is demographic changes in the workforce, projected by the U.S. Census Bureau to approach 70 per cent women and people of color by 2030. We see the message of these trends as one challenge with two dimensions: companies need to build an infrastructure that maximizes the potential of each employee, while at the same time spotlighting the issues of truly welcoming all diverse groups in the workplace and truly valuing their contributions.

As we have pointed out in previous chapters, failing to develop the potential of every employee is an intolerable waste that is limiting the productivity of companies overall. Even more compelling, diversity is already a fact throughout the industrialized world, and its impact on the workforce will mirror those demographic changes. This message applies compellingly in the rest of the world as well, where ethnic rivalries in societies and in the workplace reflect analogous experience. Peter Drucker predicted in *Management Challenges for the 21st Century* that inclusion will become a matter of "survival," and we agree. Companies that do not learn to leverage those differences for the good of the business will be left behind by those that do.

A third major trend is increasing corporate involvement in the global economy, where diversity as it has been defined in the west is the normal experience. As more and more corporations accept the business value of inclusion, they in turn put strong pressure on their vendors to do the same. We heard this story from a board member for an international manufacturer. His company had made the decision to drastically reduce its list of law firm vendors, from 300 to 30. A leading criterion for retaining the business relationship was the law firm's experience in international business. A law firm packed with friends of his, which had done business with his company for decades, was among those dropped. Diversity and inclusion suddenly became real to him: "It was time to do something about inclusion instead of just talking about it." Inclusion can no longer be dismissed as "the same old affirmative action with a new name."

Seen through this strategic lens, inclusion and development belong as a part of a company's strategic business plan, not a separate side issue, "the right thing to do" in good times. In fact, we strongly believe an organization's success as the twenty-first century progresses will depend on its ability to develop all employees within an inclusive environment. The service economy will continue to solidify, global competition will continue to intensify, and diverse populations will increase their representation in the workforce. Engaged employees who represent and/or value broader diversity in the workforce and markets, and who continuously bring their new ideas to their companies, will increasingly provide the only competitive advantage.

CUSTOMIZE THE BUSINESS CASE

The business case on a macro level is compelling, but it will not necessarily convince everyone, including many line managers, that "this applies to our company." Senior leaders have to go further, specifying the critical inclusion message. Of course, this message needs to be delivered in conjunction with key departments, like human resources, sales and marketing, which have or can acquire relevant data and experience to link inclusive behavior to a company's daily business life. Each organization has its own strategies and challenges in recruitment and retention, marketing and sales—current and potential—and its own strategy for accessing the global economy.

Nevertheless, there are common concerns and common analyses which can guide all companies in developing their individual business case for inclusion and development.

Customizing Your Business Case for an Inclusive Culture of Development

1. What is the average cost of recruitment for employees at different levels, and what does it cost to replace an employee who has left?

2. What is your turnover rate by level, by department, and for specific diversity groups? Is this an acceptable rate of turnover, given your costs of replacement and the turnover rates of your competition, as much as you can learn, or for your industry sector? How might inclusion initiatives improve your turnover rates in all these areas?

3. How long does it typically take for new employees in various areas of your company to become productive contributors?

4. How do you compare with your competition in terms of gaining market share in emerging markets? What is your current market share—regionally, nationally and globally—and in what ways might inclusion initiatives expand it? Could you become better able to recognize and access new markets? Could you become more flexible in spotting and responding to new opportunities? Are you ready to become the company Procter & Gamble CEO A. G. Lafley envisions, one that "out thinks, out-innovates and out-performs the competition"?

5. What does your data tell you about customer satisfaction? In what ways is that data influenced by inclusion and development? For example, how does the demographic profile of your employee population compare to your customer profiles or your employees' skills in interacting with diverse customers?

6. What are the potential costs—in terms of money and reputation—to inclusion-related grievances and lawsuits?

7. Do you as a leader have access to information from diverse sources? Do you engage in candid conversations about the health of the business with people who see the world from a different perspective? Do you value those different perspectives? Are you comfortable in those conversations? Are you able to learn from them and apply that learning to your business?

Once you have explored the answers to these and other questions that relate specifically to your business, you can build a business case that provides a convincing argument for inclusion and development as well as concrete goals, objectives and targets for your strategic plan.

COMMUNICATE THE BUSINESS CASE

Once your organization's specific business case is developed, it needs to be endorsed, promoted and communicated by all senior leaders, especially the CEO. As with any other critical corporate initiative, the business case for inclusion and the corresponding business plan must bear the personal stamp of the CEO and the leadership team.

How do company leaders communicate the strong, clear, critical business message of inclusion and development to all employees? We find that once an inclusive environment becomes a business priority, leaders find endless opportunities: memos, e-blasts, pronouncements and company newsletters, at staff, board and shareholder meetings, on the company Web site, during speeches to outside organizations or casual conversations with the senior team or with any employee, even in the elevator or the halls.

Personal experiences and insights add power to the business message. Getting to know a broader range of employees through formal or informal mentoring programs or rotational assignments are two common strategies. One CEO talks about how he began to see the organization differently as a result of a conversation he had with a valued African-American junior executive who had announced he was leaving the company.

When I learned how long it had taken him to reach his current position in comparison with our "fast track" people, and then when he said that he didn't see any advancement opportunities here because "no one above me looks like me," I suddenly "got it." My regret is that it didn't happen sooner. At our next executive staff meeting I began by saying, "Everyone around this table looks like me, and that needs to change."

Another executive likes to tell the story of bringing his very observant six-year-old daughter to work one day.

It was her first time in my new department, so I gave her the tour. At the end she turned to me and asked, "Daddy, how come all the people in the big offices are men and all the people in the cubbies are women?" I was stunned and didn't have an answer. I'm working on getting one, or even better, building a department where no one will ask that question again.

These are examples of the personal tone that executives who are truly committed bring to the conversation, a tone that can make all the difference for employees. All your words, written and spoken, can advance the issue, and your efforts will better attune you to the special sensitivities of those groups traditionally disenfranchised in or excluded from the workplace as well as older workers, who frequently find themselves excluded today. So they, too, will be convinced that the company is finally taking inclusion seriously.

Leaders must become so attuned to the message of inclusion and development that they always mention it, because the absence of words sends a powerful negative message. If a senior leader doesn't mention profit every time he talks, no one assumes he stopped being concerned about it.   But if a leader doesn't mention inclusion, people's antennae go up. One HR executive explained it this way.

> Some people immediately leap to the conclusion, "He no longer cares." I urge them, "Let's not get rabbit ears, like baseball umpires do, thinking they hear players saying disrespectful things." Sometimes a player can't even say "good morning" without getting thrown out of the game. But I understand the sensitivity—I try to keep in my head that missteps are magnified ten times.

LEARN WHAT'S GOING ON AT YOUR COMPANY

Most senior leaders are aware of general surveys showing the large percentage of employees—in many surveys a majority—who are not completely engaged with their work, who go through the motions rather than "bringing their brains to work." They are also aware that the responses of certain groups are even more negative. But why? Many senior leaders are effectively isolated from what happens on a daily basis in their companies because of the very nature of a hierarchy, as well as by pressing quarterly demands. Do you know what's going on in your company?

Senior leaders are likely to operate in a bubble unless they specifically seek out information. The isolation can result from a detail as small as riding an executive elevator or eating only in an executive dining room. It can happen because the network of those who report directly to you only tell you what they think you want to hear, to protect themselves as well as to avoid your displeasure. Or the problem may go deeper: your direct reports may themselves prefer to assume things are fine by choosing not to hear or listen to negative information or pointed questions. In any case, you will not be receiving the information you need.

Do you know what most of your employees, those who are not among the select few identified as high potential, experience in your company, or do you ride a metaphoric executive elevator? We can't tell you anything you don't already know about the cost of being wrong if you assume everything is fine. That's the mistake made by one CEO we work with, after he was urged out of retirement by an influential board member to turn around an underperforming company. From his positions as a leader at other major companies, this CEO had a reputation for valuing an inclusive work environment. In his new post he quite reasonably relied on his direct reports to handle the ongoing business while he developed a new success strategy for the company. He was stunned less than a year into his tenure to receive a letter signed by his most senior African-American managers detailing concerns about lack of promotions. His direct reports had not taken those questions and complaints seriously for years. Now he had to deal directly with their concerns. Going public would not only embarrass the company and harm its business, it would also embarrass him personally.

Valuable energy had to be diverted from the company's turn-around strategy to resolve issues that never would have arisen had the managers' concerns been addressed in the first place. On the positive side, this energy was put to good use repairing the working trust between upper management and the new CEO. The result is that more culture change occurred in the nine months following the letter than in the seven previous years, including a significant reduction in turnover for disenfranchised groups, new promotions and management accountability for development planning. If you commit to inclusion, such challenges become opportunities to speed progress.

The consequences of not knowing can range from this kind of wasted energy to serious business damage from public and media attention. Senior managers do not want to learn about problems through a lawsuit, a threat of a strike, injuries to consumers, underperformance of a particular unit or any other public or quasi-public occurrence. Doesn't it really make more sense to create a more hospitable work environment? We're not talking rocket science here; we're talking basic management techniques, with conscious efforts to include historically underrepresented groups as well as the vast majority of employees who are not on the traditional fast track. Don't think of all these people as "other"; include them all in your organization's development strategy.

EXAMINE WHERE YOU ARE

You can choose to know what's happening to all the employees in your company, and you can do it quickly. Here are some examples of data you can examine to find out what's really going on. This information can also serve as a baseline from which to compare data as your inclusion initiative progresses.

1. **Turnover Rates**

   With groups that have traditionally been excluded from opportunities, the belief that your workplace is not welcoming is most definitively expressed by disengagement from the work—just "getting by"—and by voluntary separation. The economic cost of turnover is substantial and easy to calculate. Just add up recruiting and training expenses, as well as the intangible but very real costs like disruption in working relationships with colleagues and clients, and damage to the company's reputation. Those numbers command attention; that's a clear business case. Investigate the reasons those people are leaving, and address their concerns. More often than not, disproportionately high turnover among disenfranchised groups is an early warning, indicating that many other employees are probably experiencing dissatisfaction as well.

What is the turnover experience at your company? Are there any patterns that can be traced back to specific departments or even specific managers? In addition, does a higher percentage of certain groups leave? Is it safe to assume it's just because they got a better job, had to follow a spouse or significant other, or simply preferred to stay home with young children? Another HR executive vice-president believes he knows the reason: "The assumption that the playing field is level—that's a faulty assumption." You need to know if frustration because of obstacles in your work environment is playing a role in people's decisions to leave.

2. Employee Surveys

How do your employees as a whole feel about working at your company and their chances for advancement? Are the perceptions of the majority of employees different from the perspective of the select few?

3. Recruitment

What is the ratio of interviews to offers among all diverse groups? How many of them accept? Do you know the reputation of your company on diversity and inclusion? How do the ratios of interviews, offers and acceptances for those in the preferred group, white men in the West, compare to those for members of disenfranchised groups? Is there a difference?

4. Internal Sourcing

Does your company have a reputation for promoting from within? Does it offer development opportunities across the board? How seriously are internal candidates considered, especially in the case of traditionally excluded groups? What is the ratio of successful applicants for promotion among those groups? Is the ratio different for those in the preferred group, the traditional source of the select few?

5. Performance Management

Does your company make sure all employees get assignments that expose them to a broad range of issues and people within the company, the necessary building blocks for promotion and success? A chief inclusion and development officer who reports directly to his CEO states what most people realize: "Corporate America has been around long enough for us to see the pattern. We know that exposure is what really advances your career."

Also, how do the overall performance ratings of members of disenfranchised groups compare to those of members of the preferred group, for example, white men in the West? Do they receive the same quality of feedback and development planning as others? How do the promotion ratios for disenfranchised groups compare to those for members of the preferred group?

6. Succession Planning

Are diverse groups represented in the plan? If they are, do they receive the kind of development opportunities that will prepare them for executive positions, or do they stay in the "ready in three to five years" category?

Whether the results of your audit are surprisingly good or disappointing, you know what to do. Study each situation, devise a strategy for change, including replicating what does work, and then monitor progress. And we're never surprised to find that just a question from a senior leader can start the change process.

PREPARE A COMPREHENSIVE STRATEGIC PLAN

Once you know what your current situation is, you are ready to establish specific inclusion and development goals and lay them out in a strategic plan. What procedures will make change happen? People issues, whether interpersonal or organizational, can seldom if ever be solved by a blanket initiative, especially one that tries to convince all staff of the general importance of treating all employees with respect. "Going through the motions" is glib and unsatisfactory for all and insulting to many, and scattershot approaches yield little in the way of results.

There is no advantage gained, for example, from a series of awareness training sessions that are not connected to a realignment of company policies and practices with the business objective of developing the potential of all employees. Just as with every other aspect of business, the way to achieve concrete results is to identify specific issues and then address them in a systematic manner. As with any other company-wide initiative, the leadership must commit the necessary resources. If all major company initiatives are rolled out by the CEO with a marketing blitz, periodic course corrections, and accountability for results, and diversity and inclusion initiatives are not, the workplace message of low priority is what's heard, no matter how supportive the words in the speeches or written directives. The point is not to throw money at inclusion but to treat it as you would any other business priority.

People can and do read unspoken messages. A long-time successful account executive knows most employees see through to the truth: "If you look at the senior leadership team and you don't see a plan that is truly in action, there's nobody different there, the rest is just words."

SUPPORT ROLE MODELS AT THE TOP

A common statement among disenfranchised groups in the U.S. is that they come up against a glass or even concrete ceiling at work. They are inspired if even one person "like them" has broken through to the leadership team, and we know the metaphor resonates with all other diverse groups around the world who suffer similar exclusion. We have found, time after time, that good intentions alone are not enough to bring about those breakthroughs. Someone already on the leadership team has to decide to be proactive, so why not you? Explained one executive vice-president of HR:

> *Putting a woman or person of color on the board or on the executive team makes a statement without words, giving people hope that they can move up the ladder. It also*

demonstrates management's commitment is serious.
It's one thing to mandate diversity over there, but quite
another to live with it in your own small group.

But the real value of the role model organizationally comes
from its ability to inspire further progress, when others in the
company identify with the behavior and begin to promote more
members of diverse groups. That same VP continues,

Role models create pressure to change throughout the
company. Everyone starts to feel pressure to make other
people successful. It becomes self-fulfilling.

LEAD BY EXAMPLE

Role models are important symbols, but the enduring signals
about cultural change spring from the personal involvement
of all leaders, involvement that is consistent and sustained over
time. That means thinking strategically about what drives change
and then beginning to make those behavior changes in your own
life.

1. **Personal Interactions**

    One of the best places to begin is by scrolling through your
    own personal interactions, both within the company and
    outside it. Who are the people you have lunch with or meet
    with to strategize or analyze what's important to your busi-
    ness? Are all the people like you, or do they represent di-
    verse groups? What is your interaction with your board on
    the subject of inclusion? Does the board have champions of

diversity and inclusion? What about coaching, mentoring and sponsoring colleagues? Were members of diverse groups among those who benefited from your experience, or were the beneficiaries mostly younger white men? Put a diversity screen on your interactions, just to see what they look like.

2. Positioning and Promotion Decisions

Over the last fifteen years or so, who were the people you personally hired or promoted from within? Were any members of diverse groups among them? Did you have a diverse candidate pool? Did you ever stop a selection process because it did not contain diverse candidates? If your answer to any of these questions is no, is it that you decided none were qualified? Or is it just that you did not think about it? Do you recognize and reward your people for inclusive behavior or for developing others?

Does your succession planning include diverse candidates? If you do decide to propose a member of a diverse group for the list, are you willing to remain steady when others question your choice? Will you withstand the pressure, no matter how good-natured or couched in teasing it is, or will you back down? Will you go a step further and investigate why the other person is pushing back? Is it just discomfort with change? People in the queue have a vested interest in maintaining the status quo. They are more comfortable when their competition is "like" them, and they don't want to be confused by people they don't feel they know or understand. Again, there's no value to attaching negative judgment to these questions or their answers. We all need a push to start experiencing the view through different lenses.

3. Community Involvement

Most senior leaders lend their time, talent and treasure to not-for-profit organizations, and these, too, can be opportunities to signal a changed level of commitment. Which organizations do you choose to champion, and what kinds of change do they work for? What is the nature of your personal involvement, and how deep does it reach?

RATE YOURSELF

Once you have answers to at least some of these questions, give yourself an overall rating. On a scale of one to ten, with ten being a champion of diversity and inclusion, how would you rate your behavior? Do you see a benefit to your business if you move that needle a little closer to ten? How far do you want the shadow of your leadership to stretch?

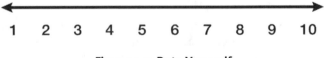

Figure 4.1: Rate Yourself

As a result of doing this audit, senior leaders sometimes realize that their personal interactions involve more diversity than they thought, and this raises the level of their commitment. Others realize how narrow the range of people with whom they interact is and begin to seek more opportunities. There is no judgment attached to either of these realizations; it simply confirms the difficulty of integrating diversity and inclusion into our lives. It doesn't just happen, and it doesn't just happen in the workplace either.

LOOK THROUGH A DIFFERENT LENS

Up to this point we have focused on the concrete actions that senior leaders can take to build an inclusive culture of development. But there is another critical component to being an authentic champion of inclusion—having the ability to view situations "through a different lens" in order to more fully understand how people who are different from you experience the world. This added insight will make you even more effective as a change agent. In addition, your people will realize that you are leading not just from the head but also from the heart, and your credibility will be strengthened.

As a leader, you are the role model for others. But what will help you, the leader, overcome your own implicit biases and assumptions? One of the best ways to make your implicit beliefs explicit so that you can examine them is to immerse yourself for extended periods of time in another culture. Soon things you once considered "common sense" are understood as being just one of several options, and perhaps not the best option in all circumstances. Overseas assignments have provided this learning experience for many of our clients. Here is the surprising lesson of one senior manager.

I was sent to a small city in southern Europe to manage one of our factories. My management philosophy focused on the importance of empowering employees by involving them in decision-making whenever this was appropriate. After about three months, one of the local supervisors came to me very concerned about the morale of the workers. He explained that by asking for input and trying to involve employees, I had created the impression that I was incompetent. According to local logic, a competent manager would know what to do—after all, that's why he was the manager. I soon realized that, while I still wanted employee input, I would have to find culturally appropriate ways to get it.

Although many senior leaders may never have this cross-cultural experience at work, most will encounter people different from themselves in their professional and personal lives. We know a CEO who used to be an executive at an airline company. He often traveled with another executive who was African-American, and they became friends. By traveling together, he saw firsthand the Negative Treatment his friend received, even from employees in his own company. These experiences helped him understand the exclusion that people of color experience in a way that just hearing or reading about it would not. As a result, he was better able to relate to the concerns of people of color in the workplace and champion their inclusion, even though he was not one of them.

The lesson of understanding can also come in reverse, where a white man finds himself in circumstances that make him feel excluded. One senior executive we know remembers a meeting at a subsidiary in Ireland, where he didn't understand one thing they were talking about, even though they were speaking English: "I don't think I felt the full weight of what women and people of color feel, but I got a taste of it."

A now-retired CEO often talks of his participation in the civil rights marches in the South and the impact it had on how he ran his company. Another continues to be motivated by his mother's experience in a Nazi death camp. And increased societal openness, in housing, in school, and in the workplace, has brought similar enlightenment to those who have no personal experience with traumatic socio-political events. Sons and daughters have brought home friends and, more challenging, spouses from different backgrounds. Despite the resistance, fear and worry, the changes have brought acceptance and, in most cases, insight into the experiences of others. After these personal encounters, the requests, opinions and even demands of disenfranchised and diverse groups at work can be seen for what they really are: legitimate efforts to better their situations—wake-up calls, not threats. They are constructive feedback, opportunities to improve a company's practices, and these improvements will result in better performance overall.

Some of the most effective teachers on the topic of the subtle tendencies to exclude have been the daughters of senior leaders. When their daughters encounter barriers at work, fathers tend to take another look at their own companies. We know one CEO whose daughter received degrees from top schools and then was hired in an impressive sales job at a pharmaceutical company. On a visit home she burst into tears, describing her treatment by her colleagues. They ignored her at meetings and ridiculed her for not playing golf. Her father's response? "I've heard the same story from women in my company for years, and I never paid any attention to them." Things began to change at his company.

Another CEO's daughter described to her parents her difficulty finding quality child care as she prepared to return to work. She said to her father, "I hope your employees don't have to go through the same struggle." At that time many of his women employees had in fact been pushing for child care, but its importance didn't hit his radar screen until his daughter had trouble finding a suitable environment for his grandchild. That up-close-and-personal experience can enable you to see things differently. Before long, his company had an on-site child care center.

Even if you haven't had any of these experiences, as a senior leader you can create many opportunities to interact with people different from yourself in situations where your goal is to learn from them. For example, some companies have established "reverse mentoring" programs so that senior leaders can learn skills that seem to come naturally to younger employees. A frequent example is using high-tech equipment effectively. In these exchanges, senior leaders can gain personal insight into the feelings, thoughts and experiences of employees who view the world from a different perspective. Other senior leaders make it a point to have lunch at least once a month with groups of diverse employees. In this and similar "reaching-out" workplace activities, it's crucial that the leader come with an open and inquiring mind, focus on listening, but also be willing to share any relevant personal experiences.

SECURE YOUR LEGACY

We know from our experience that many senior leaders are troubled by the lack of progress in achieving inclusion and a culture of development, even after more than three decades of time, money and energy spent on special programs. These leaders are not opposed to workforce changes; in fact, they want change. They genuinely believe their companies are meritocracies, fair and open to all, and they feel confused and frustrated by the slow pace of progress among employees who represent traditionally disenfranchised groups. Behavior change, as Kelman and Hamilton declared long ago, is not achieved by either the best intentions or simply spending money.

Many leaders, as they approach retirement, find themselves thinking about their legacies, much like heads of state contemplating their place in history as they come to the end of their terms in office. Maturity and experience give leaders a broader perspective on world events, their organization, the nature of change, and their own accomplishments. Issues that don't fit into the "bottom line" formula for producing quarterly earnings but are clearly crucial to future success can capture serious effective attention. We believe creating an inclusive organization is one such issue. For example, we know of one company that was featured on the cover of a major industry magazine, and all of their "players" on the cover were white men. One of their large clients who had a strong commitment to inclusion was outraged at the fact that the face of their key vendor was entirely white and male. The client decided to take a major chunk of its business elsewhere. The vendor company's CEO had been talking about doing better with inclusion for years, but the loss of business finally got his attention. As a result, he became much more aggressive about building an inclusive organization as his legacy.

Have you been focused on quarterly earnings? Perhaps as you approach retirement you can feel freer to devote resources to longer-term investments, for example in people development. Peter Drucker suggests in *Management Challenges for the 21st Century* that a focus on quarterly earnings is always too narrow a perspective. Who are the shareholders who demand those quarterly earnings anyway? To a very great degree they are employees everywhere saving for their retirements two or more decades down the road, individually or collectively as institutional investors. Shareholders do want quarterly increases, but they also are banking on the long-term success of the company. Are those spectacular quarterly earnings from Enron of any value to the shareholders now? Balancing those seemingly competing goals requires different organizational decisions and strategies, and you may be the one to chart the new course.

Many companies in consumer product industries are already at or close to reaching that business conclusion, and the logic is beginning to work its way into the plans of business-to-business enterprises. Two energy company executive vice-presidents we know say the same thing, even though they operate on opposite ends of the globe: "A company of all-white engineers has done well and can still be successful today, but that strategy is not sustainable." We will need maximum performance from all our employees. Is it enough to belittle the challenges from diverse groups, saying, "Give us more time," or, worse, to deny they exist, saying, "We don't have a problem"?

If you are nearing retirement, your personal success is secure, and you can probably afford to look into a future beyond the next quarterly returns. You certainly know how to bring about organizational change, so you are in a position to secure your company's future performance by establishing a culture of development today.

Business leaders may not be able to change the world, but they can effect dramatic change within their own businesses. Creating business processes that are rock-solid responses to current realities and fact-based future projections is quite a legacy. And it is within reach. As society tries to push us all into narrower and narrower pigeonholes, we realize that none of us really fit. We are all unique, but at the deepest level of our values and our yearnings, we are far more similar than we are different. An obvious way to capitalize on those similarities is to work together to achieve business success. This is the value to be internalized.

CHAPTER FIVE

Aligning Human Resources With A Culture Of Development

Inclusion is not a separate activity. It's an integral part of the things we do day in and day out. When you talk about a performance appraisal, you build in inclusion; when you give feedback, when you talk about goal setting and salary, you build in inclusion. That's the next level.

Carlos Perea
Executive Vice-President
Bell South Latin America

If a company assumes, even unconsciously, that only a few are talented, it would not be surprising if human resources (HR) concentrated attention on those talented few and ignored or neglected the rest. Indeed, when we look closely at most HR systems, we find that they reinforce a "Castes in Concrete" model of development. While the goal of HR should be to maximize effort on behalf of the company's business objectives, HR policies and procedures that stem from "Castes in Concrete" assumptions actually limit the contributions of most employees. Without guidance or support, most employees are left on their own to decide what effort they will apply to their work, and how much. The result for the company is waste: lower productivity, demoralized employees and excessive turnover.

What do employees in general feel about the significance of HR in their careers? Our focus group and survey data indicate that most employees are less than enthusiastic.

> *I don't even know who my HR representative is. I'm not sure what they do other than send us information about benefits.*

> *HR always sides with management, never with us. I don't trust them.*

> *I've applied for several jobs that HR has posted, but half the time they already know who they want and just post the jobs because they have to.*

In our experience, inclusion and a culture of development can only thrive in combination with a strategic or forward-thinking human resources function. This involves redefining HR from its traditional administrative and support role to that of a strategic partner with leaders in planning the company's future and with line managers in developing all employees.

This chapter clarifies specific actions a strategic HR department can take to build and sustain a culture of development for all employees. We begin by discussing why and how organizations can develop objective performance standards that provide the necessary foundation for defining development goals and assessing performance. We then look at how those standards, along with other inclusive strategies, can be integrated into five key HR processes that affect employees at five critical points of contact during their work history:

1. Recruitment and selection;
2. On-boarding of new hires;
3. Performance management;
4. Internal sourcing, both lateral and promotional; and
5. Succession planning.

DEVELOPING OBJECTIVE STANDARDS

The first step is for HR professionals, leaders and managers to partner in developing clear and objective standards of performance that can be used in recruiting, coaching and mentoring, as well as in performance management and promotion decisions. In companies where standards are vague and implicit, the key decisions affecting employees' work lives are often based on subjectivity rather than objective criteria. Even worse, most employees have little realistic understanding of what skills they need to develop and what behaviors they need to exhibit in order to succeed. It's not just individual employees who are confused; managers don't know what to say or do either. One client described her frustration as she tried to figure out how she could improve her performance.

In my annual review I was rated "Meets Standards" in
all areas. I asked my manager what I needed to do to get
rated "Exceeds Standards," and he told me to go to HR
with my question. HR gave me some general guidelines,
but they really didn't answer my question. I still don't
know what I have to do.

Many, if not most, employees are in the same position.
They do not know what it really takes to succeed in a particular company, and their managers don't know how to guide them.
Personnel decisions seem to be based on who you know or whether your manager feels comfortable with you. The possibility of
such unproductive speculation, to our mind, actually makes the
case for objective performance standards.

There are two categories of performance standards that
employees need to be aware of. We refer to them as "technical
competencies" and "behavioral competencies."

Technical, Job-specific Competencies

The technical requirements of your job—for example, how to use
an Excel spreadsheet—are relatively easy to understand. They are
often part of the job description, are readily available to all, and
performance of them is usually quantifiable. Can you now manipulate data on an Excel spreadsheet so we can plan budgets and
keep track of expenses? Can you control product quality better
now on that new machine? Can you make a better PowerPoint
presentation? Can you write a more convincing proposal or a
better report? Most managers and employees understand these
competencies, and work is organized around accomplishing the
specific tasks or outcomes they list. Moreover, most companies

are willing to provide technical training to employees, both in house and off-site.

Behavioral Competencies

As most employees have learned, mastering the technical competencies is only Step One. A complete answer to the question "What do I need to do to succeed?" includes not only technical competencies but also something more. That "extra something" is called by many different names: people skills, leadership skills, qualities, values. We call them "Behavioral Competencies." These are the behaviors that are most valued by the organization in all employees, regardless of job title. Behavioral competencies are the unwritten rules about success in a particular company, and they cut across all jobs and all levels. Some employees are instantly aware of these standards; others learn them from mentors; and still others figure them out on their own over years of trial and error, by watching successful people in the company and trying to model what they do.

Many employees, however, are either unaware of them or wrongly disdain them as "politics." These employees will all miss the opportunity to develop the skills that really make the difference between success and mediocrity. Emphatically, these competencies are never small, subtle or unimportant parts of any job; even in highly technical jobs, they are critical. Imagine a systems engineer who plans poorly, or a financial analyst who communicates poorly with management. These are not issues that can be overlooked. If you think back to people who were poor performers in your organization, you'll probably note that their shortcomings were more often in these behavioral areas, not the technical areas.

Behavioral competencies fall roughly into three categories: generally applicable leadership skills, skills that apply differently in different settings or functions, and skills that apply differently at different levels.

- Examples of generally applicable leadership skills are Planning and Organizing (able to create detailed project plans, balance the need for adequate planning with the need for action, and use resources efficiently) or Resilience (able to remain calm and professional in potentially volatile interactions, maintain high productivity in stressful situations, and view failures objectively and rebound quickly). These skills apply across the board, to most jobs and functions at most levels.
- Examples of skills that apply differently in different settings or functions are Customer Focus (Retail) (able to be positive with and show appreciation toward customers at all times and demonstrate unwavering politeness and courtesy) as compared to "Customer Focus" (Home Improvement) (able to seek full understanding of customer needs and match offerings to those needs and implement services in a way that meets customer needs and maximizes customer satisfaction).
- Examples of skills that apply differently at different levels are Teamwork (Individual Contributor) (able to complete own share of the team's work and support team decisions, even if different from own opinion), Teamwork (Local Leadership) (able to coach others in building team relationships and involve others as appropriate in making decisions on behalf of the team), and Teamwork (Organizational Leadership) (able to create organizational culture, systems and processes that enable cross-functional teamwork while resolving boundary issues between departments).

With this basic understanding of behavioral competencies, we now move on to the strategies HR and management can employ to make the competencies explicit. In our experience, the best results are achieved through a collaborative process among knowledgeable people within each organization. One Fortune 500 company we work with undertook this process several years ago. The executive vice-president of HR described the process.

> We first concentrated on getting common terms. My hope was to reduce everything to eight behavioral competencies, but we finally established twelve. We've tested them throughout the organization, and I think we can reasonably measure them objectively.

From his words, it is clear the process was longer than he had hoped or expected, but happily concluded. What are the steps behind his happy conclusion? We have found the following steps distinguish the most effective processes:

1. **Interviews with Senior Executives** to identify the organization's specific business goals and objectives over the next few years and to determine the behavioral competencies people in the organization will need to support them. For example, if the organization is moving toward increased responsiveness to customers, "decisiveness" is a competency its people should develop. Making decisions quickly based on good judgment and available information would serve that effort. Or, if the organization is moving toward innovative solutions, "creativity" would be an important competency. Pursuing out-of-the-box approaches would go a long way in such an environment.

2. **Focus Groups with Other High Performers** across all sections and levels of the organization to capture different information and different perspectives. The competencies that foster success in one part of the organization may be different in other areas. For example, engineering and finance jobs depend on "Attention to Detail," but it is not the same priority in marketing.

3. **Selection of a Credible Competency Inventory.** A number of companies have created proprietary competency lists which are well defined, actionable, and redundancy resistant. These lists often include a user-friendly method of identifying the top competencies for any given job or family of jobs and then prioritizing them. For example, one company list has twenty-two behavioral competencies and a prioritizing tool that helps companies identify the six to ten most important ones for that particular company. The key is to train your people in how to use these tools effectively. "Eyeballing" will not achieve an effective result.

    These lists enable companies to capitalize on the experience of others rather than having to reinvent the wheel. But the whole list will seldom apply at any one company, so it will still need customizing. In other words, companies cannot shortcut the entire deliberative process. But such lists, if used wisely, can jump-start the process.

4. **A Trained Specialist to Provide Guidance and Integration.** Who will conduct the interviews and focus groups, look for commonalities and define the competencies in appropriate detail? We recommend a trained specialist, because lack of training can result in competencies which are biased, filtered through a "move quickly" lens or a "follow rules" lens,

or lacking in enough concreteness to guide action. For example, what does "demonstrate creativity" mean? Should an employee suggest new ideas? Act on new ideas without first verifying them with management? Do something different even though the existing procedure worked well?

The trained specialist will be able to avoid these pitfalls as well as the issues of redundancy and lack of differentiation.

- Redundancy. A common concept appears in multiple competencies. The result is competencies with blurry purpose, so they are less able to guide action. For example, "Create and maintain a fun work environment" could be placed under "Teamwork," where its intent would be relatively clear. But if it is put under "Teamwork," "Innovation," "Commitment," *and* "Communication," most employees would be confused about the required behavior. Trained specialists can engineer around this pitfall.
- Lack of differentiation. A master set of competencies does not differentiate across levels or functions. Unfortunately, a competency that applies to many levels and functions will necessarily be vague and thus confuse many employees. Trained specialists have solutions, such as a small list of competencies that applies to everybody, with subsets that apply to different levels and functions according to their differing priorities. Retail, for example, may put "Decisiveness" at the top of its list, while Operations focuses on "Analytical Problem Solving." A second option is completely different competency lists for each department, or even each job.

5. **Consensus building and testing**. Once the first round of information integration is complete, the original contributors

and others should review the competency list and discuss next steps. This is the beginning of an iterative process, at first very amorphous and new. It is most unlikely the first competency list will be the final one, the best practices. Even once there is agreement on a list, it should be reviewed at least annually to accommodate internal and external landscape evolution.

If developing behavioral competencies seems like a large undertaking, you are correct. The steps we have outlined can minimize the very real problem of time and the lesser problem of expense. There is no one list of competencies, although there is frequent overlap and agreement, and there is no one way to institute competencies across a company. What is needed is the commitment to objective standards, because an inclusive culture of development is not possible without them. The goal is to be consistent, clear and appropriate, or employees will not understand how to apply them and will therefore fall back on continuing their usual behavior—"the way we've always done things."

The next step is integrating behavioral competencies into the five critical points of contact we have identified between employees and the organization.

RECRUITMENT AND SELECTION

Typically, recruitment and selection are an employee's first point of contact with any company. Effective recruitment and the selection decisions that follow should begin with a diverse team of recruiters trained in behavioral interviewing techniques, including how to interview across differences and assess candidates based on objective standards rather than instincts or gut reactions.

Sourcing Candidates

Where do companies look for candidates? To begin with, companies have to make a conscious decision to search proactively for a diverse pool of candidates. This means moving beyond traditional sources, and most companies have done so. Recruiters now routinely go to many more schools, both undergraduate and graduate, many more professional associations, including those representing diverse candidates, and tap into many more informal networks than they did in the past.

In addition, some companies have established opportunities for summer and year-round internships, where the entire experience can almost be seen as a very long job interview. Slates *(Aday kotes)* have become far more diverse, and HR can monitor selection results with ease. The goal of an inclusive process is to hire more diverse candidates, not just to interview them or provide them with summer internships.

A strategic HR department can exercise a large measure of control over recruiting results for diverse candidates, but recruiters do not operate in a vacuum. Their companies' reputations precede them. Many diverse candidates have become savvy at discerning in advance which companies are likely to be hospitable to their efforts. Often the clearest signal to them is the presence or absence of people like themselves in leadership positions. One former HR executive remembers his own difficulty in recruiting people of color on college campuses when his company had few, if any, role models.

They'd ask me, "What are the opportunities for growth into top management?" I knew what they meant. It was difficult to talk honestly and convincingly about opportunity, given the lack of progress over the company's 150-year history. The statistical truth is that it might never happen.

Another woman we know remembers how she selected between two offers after day-long interviews at the end of business school.

At both I saw only white men, but at one there were a few mustaches and even a beard, and a few tweed and plaid suits. Not much diversity, but I thought I stood a better chance of doing something there.

Recruiters who understand those concerns and can convey a deep company commitment to changing the current situation through an inclusive culture of development will be better able to sell their companies to all candidates.

Recognizing and Eliminating Subjective Assumptions

The challenge of moving beyond the unconscious tendencies that influence assessment decisions is described perfectly by one long-term HR executive.

Unless I'm consciously looking to expand my world, I will always hire myself. It's a very natural force: "I like myself. I do a hell of a job. If I could just find another me, I'd jump at the chance." The problem with this approach is that it doesn't enable me to see all the other people who could

*do as well or better than I can, who just happen to look
or act differently.*

The challenge of inclusion is broadening that perspective
to include the underlying qualities, and not just the physical or
cultural resemblance to the recruiter. Conscious intervention is
usually necessary to achieve a diverse workforce and to leverage
that workforce into an inclusive work environment, to make the
differences work for the company.

To maximize inclusiveness, interviewers should be on the
lookout for these common examples of bias.

Interviewer Red Flags

- *Similar to me*—The interviewer has something
  in common with the candidate, such as attend-
  ing the same school, and therefore thinks the
  candidate will be a high performer. Or, imagine the
  excitement a manager will feel to learn that a candidate likes the same baseball team. Perhaps an
  immediate spark will fly, creating a positive bias.
  However, the candidate may be sorely lacking (or
  worse, slightly lacking, thus making detection more
  difficult) in key competencies.

- *Halo effect*—The interviewer assumes that a candidate's strength in one area will translate to strength
  in another unrelated area; for example, she has
  strong computer skills, so she is probably great at
  problem-solving. Or, an interviewer may conclude

that a candidate has good judgment in choosing among options, and erroneously conclude that the candidate is also likely to pursue rather than avoid sensitive conversations because it matches the interviewer's perception of "good judgment."

- *First impressions*—The interviewer makes a hiring decision that is too influenced by irrelevant first impressions; for example, the candidate's weak handshake probably means a bad fit. While it is indeed possible that a weak handshake may indicate a lack of confidence in some of the people some of the time, the handshake probably has minimal relevance for most jobs.

- *Pet theory*—The interviewer makes a hiring decision based not on job-related factors but on personal beliefs about what makes a good (or bad) candidate; for example, the candidate has only worked in an academic setting and the interviewer believes that ivory towers and business don't mix well. The pet theories can take many forms, and many of them will appear credible at first glance. "I won't hire anyone who worked for Company X because I don't like their methods." Or, "I prefer to hire people who get right to the point." This may reflect a social style rather than a job-related need.

- *Stereotypes*—The interviewer evaluates the individual based on assumptions and beliefs about that person's group; for example, a woman will probably start a family soon and won't be available for long. Or, "People from New York are too blunt. My customers need more coddling. Don't hire him." While these points may accurately describe some individuals, it is unproductive to assume that they describe all people in that group.

- *Hearsay*—The interviewer bases the hiring decision on unconfirmed descriptions of previous work relationships. This is especially common in evaluating internal candidates; for example, "I heard that he's not a very good team player. I don't think I'll take a chance." Or, a person might "take the fall" for a bad situation, which is a gross oversimplification of everything that happened, most of which was out of his or her control. While the hearsay might be one piece of data, it is often a very unreliable, untrue or inappropriately skewed piece of data.

Many companies have found they can avoid the impact of these red flag behaviors in recruitment and selection by having panels of diverse interviewers and reviewers who have acquired the skill to interact with and evaluate objectively across differences, both visible and invisible. This applies not just to the recruiting team, but also to everyone involved in the interviewing process. But how might they get those skills? One good answer is training. The training can be general, and cut across purposes, or it can relate to specific functions, such as recruiting or interviewing. Such training can be designed in-house or it can be purchased from established companies. Purchasing it from established companies may be more expensive in terms of direct costs, but it will be much faster than designing it in-house, and is likely to be better because it has already been tested in many settings.

Behavioral Interviewing

One of the key skills the most effective interviewers use is behavioral interviewing, which we introduced in Chapter 1. Behavioral interviewing allows candidates to describe specific verifiable past behaviors that are relevant to a company's behavioral competencies. The goal of the technique is to delve deeper into a candidate's experience than a simple review of work history normally does and to assess a candidate's capacity to learn and to grow. For a company committed to a culture of development, the benefits of pursuing this recruitment strategy are apparent, and many companies provide specific training in behavioral interviewing for their recruiters.

Behavioral interviewing introduces open-ended discussions by asking questions such as:

- Describe a time when a teammate needed your assistance but you had your own pressing demands. How did you handle it?
- Think of something you did well because you had learned from past successes and failures. Please describe it and highlight how you changed your behavior as a result of what you learned.
- Some people see change as frightening, and some see it as a way to grow. Describe something you've done that illustrates how you view and treat change as a way to grow.
- Describe a situation that demonstrates how you express confidence in and show support for people equally, regardless of age, race, gender, work style or other diverse characteristic.

- Describe a time when you worked on a team made up of people with diverse perspectives or backgrounds. How did you capitalize on these differences to accomplish business objectives?

A recruiter who uses behavioral interviewing techniques would not ask a candidate questions like "What type of a team player are you?" or "How do you feel about working with a diverse group of associates?" Responses to these questions would be limited to a few words that would in no way illuminate any real skill or experience— "I enjoy working on teams," or "I'm fine with differences—I relate well to all kinds of people."

Because behavioral competencies are transferable, demonstration of experience achieving them can come from experience anywhere, not just at work. One executive described how the use of behavioral interviewing allowed his company to identify a broader base of capable employees.

Our interview process is based upon looking at people's life experiences. The premise is that people are likely to do things well in the future if they have done those same things well in the past, no matter where. The first question we ask is, "Tell me about a goal you've set and achieved in any area of your life. We want to know what it was, what you did, and what the results were." Another question is, "Give me an example of a time when you were a member of a team and persuaded your team members to take an action you wanted them to take."

His company is, in effect, basing questions on two of its behavioral competencies—efficacy and teamwork—to assess the individual's potential to contribute to the company in line with both its values and its business requirements.

As these examples demonstrate, the most effective behavioral interviewing questions are framed to reveal relevant behavior and experience in a variety of settings, since some candidates may not have had the opportunity to demonstrate all skills in the same or a similar job, or even in the workplace. Other situations might include school activities, religious or community functions, civic or non-profit organizations, sports or military service. As we have discussed, behavioral competencies are not limited to a specific job title or situation; they are transferable among many situations.

Despite the challenges of opening up recruitment and selection to diverse candidates, these activities turn out to be one of the least problematic steps in the inclusion process, and many companies have achieved impressive results. The real tests come after selection. How long do diverse candidates stay at the company? What are their actual work experiences while in the organization? Those experiences begin with on-boarding.

On-Boarding

Most companies offer new hires some form of orientation when they first arrive. Usually those sessions cover the specific requirements of their new jobs and an introduction to formal company processes, such as performance evaluations and benefits. In addition, this is the time when sorting and selecting begins—remember the manager in Chapter 2 who actually was handed a list of "winners" and "slackers"—so more is in order. These orientations, if they are so limited, we view as missed opportunities. With slight modifications, and HR working in partnership with management, companies can greatly enhance the value of on-boarding sessions.

Here are some concrete suggestons:

1. **Present and discuss the organization's behavioral competencies**—descriptions of the qualities and behaviors it values and that contribute to success within it.

2. **Introduce new hires to the important unwritten rules of the organization**. These rules can be as broad as "the way we do things around here" and as specific as dress codes or preferred formats for reports and presentations. While many may assume that these rules are too obvious to deserve special mention, we have found that they are exactly the ones that trip up many, if not most, employees. With few specific role models to observe or to turn to for advice, they often have little opportunity to learn the informal rules. A strategic HR can begin to address this disadvantage.

    In our experience, these discussions may be more open and honest if employees in the new hire's functional area and at his/her level lead them. For women and people of color, an additional plus would be to have someone like them make the presentation, either at their level or someone at a higher level who can serve as a role model of success.

3. **Communicate the company's commitment to inclusion and a culture of development**, where the success of all employees is fostered through structured development opportunities, managerial support, regular feedback on past performance, and guidance on how to improve performance in the future. Let new employees know what specific resources exist and

how they can access them. A key part of the message is a statement about the company's commitment to openness, where
employees are encouraged to report any problems, obstacles and barriers they encounter. Some describe discussions
with managers first, others with diversity officers, still others
with HR. Each company decides on its own preferred procedure.

4. **Reinforce the need for each employee to take responsibility
   for his or her own career development**, and provide some
   skill-building examples or role-playing exercises to illustrate
   the typical issues. We strongly believe in all employees taking personal responsibility for their careers, but at the same
   time we do not advocate that all of the responsibility be on
   their shoulders. Companies will enhance performance if they
   provide a welcoming environment—tools, process and training—to make good on the promise of supporting the career
   development aspirations of employees. On-boarding topics
   that prepare employees to take that responsibility are: understanding one's own and the organization's goals, getting
   mileage out of 360-degree feedback, and guiding growth-
   oriented discussion with one's manager.

PERFORMANCE MANAGEMENT

Over the last decade, many managers have begun to move beyond
an annual performance evaluation to more ongoing conversations with their staff about performance. This evolution signals
progress toward a culture of development. We applaud this strategic thinking and behavior but we do not mean by this to devalue
the more formal process. This is not an "either-or" proposition:

in fact, managers should be engaging in formal planning and reviews, along with giving ongoing feedback so that at the time of the annual review there are no surprises.

We urge HR to be forward-thinking in both the formal and informal processes. HR can provide critical structure and support to managers and employees as they continue the transition to a culture of development. The first step is establishing company-wide objective standards, and the next steps involve examining all aspects of performance management responsibilities to identify where managers can promote and reinforce the three components of a culture of development—clear objective standards of performance applied equally to all, development opportunities for all employees and constructive feedback to shape future performance.

Here are some guidelines that HR can use to facilitate an inclusive performance management process.

Evaluate Against Objective Standards

An important component of a culture of development is measuring every employee's performance against an objective standard rather than against the performance of other employees. By "objective" standards, we do not mean a numbers standard; we mean concretely defined behavioral competencies which are practical in a variety of settings. Measuring employees' performances against such an objective standard is the preferred situation, and we recommend that companies who intend to build a formal performance management system, or restructure their current system, follow this model.

At the same time, however, we realize that many companies may have already spent considerable time and resources implementing a performance management system that does, in fact, measure one person's performance against the performance of other employees. The most common name for this type of system is "forced ranking." Briefly, the theory behind forced ranking systems is that the performance of any random sample of people will fall into a bell curve, where 10 to 20 per cent excel, 10 to 20 per cent do poorly, and the remaining 60 to 80 per cent are grouped in between: the average.

There are mixed opinions about the validity of the bell curve model in ranking employees. Supporters of forced ranking say the system ensures honest evaluations and, therefore, a basis for weeding out underperformers. If managers are not forced to rank on a bell curve, they will rank everyone in the top category, avoiding hard decisions and difficult and time-consuming conversations with their direct reports.

Critics say that corporate employees, especially professionals, are not a random sample, and therefore their performance does not necessarily fall into a bell curve, with a few stars, a few failures, and most employees clustering around average performance. If the company hires the *crème de la crème*, the stated goal of its staffing processes, they may in fact have mostly excellent performers. And since the system has damaged morale, undercut teamwork, discouraged real risk-taking and resulted in so many lawsuits, critics continue, its risks will always outweigh its benefits.

In our experience most employees do not like forced ranking systems, and many managers are equally uncomfortable because they are the ones stuck delivering the bad news, too often to employees who have worked hard and made good contributions. In the words of one manager:

When I've got six people who are consistently performing at 120 per cent , how do I explain that I can only give out two "exceeds expectations"?

Another client explained what typically happens in his company around evaluation time.

Some managers engage in elaborate strategies to keep people they want, in effect neutralizing the system's supposed efficiencies. For example, people are traded among departments, or poor performers are kept on so that someone is available to sacrifice.

We recognize that there are many companies who already use some form of forced ranking for their performance management process and, as a result, we're often asked, "Can this process co-exist with the goal of building an inclusive culture of development?" The answer is a qualified yes, but only if the following are integral parts of the process, with management accountability built in.

- Published competencies, and the behaviors that demonstrate them, are the basis for discussions as well as for determining an individual's potential.
- Each cycle starts with a clean slate, that is, every employee has the same opportunity to change their relative position on the curve in each cycle.
- All employees (a) receive stretch assignments, (b) have the confidence of their manager to succeed and (c) seek and receive continuous, balanced feedback.

The forced ranking trap to avoid is allowing the same "go-to" people to get all the best assignments, because as long as they do, they will stay at the head of the curve, and no others will have an opportunity to move up. At the same time, managers have to keep a close watch on their own determinations about potential. For example, managers need to avoid defining potential as "he reminds me of me of when I was his age."

Establish Consistency

Once HR has designed the forms and formalized the process, its continuing role is to ensure that performance planning and review sessions are consistent across the company, and that managers are held accountable. One of the major problems we encounter in organizations is the lack of consistency among managers. We repeatedly hear of very different experiences from focus group participants who work in the same organization.

> Yeah, we're supposed to have a review every quarter. I haven't had one in three years. I guess no news is good news.

> My supervisor tells me to write the review, and he'll sign it.

> I must be lucky because my boss gives a thorough review to all of us. I don't know how she finds the time, but she does.

If managers are not consistently having quality performance discussions with each employee, or if they are simply "checking the box" on a form or filling in forms incorrectly, and are never called to task, the process will end up benefiting a select few and excluding most others. With consistency and accountability, the evaluations become strategic planning opportunities for managers, employees and the company as a whole.

Consistency can be achieved most efficiently if HR provides managers with specific training, including training in how to use the forms, how to deliver feedback and how to develop goals, and why consistency across employees is important. In addition, the organization must hold managers accountable for this key aspect of their job. One HR executive used a tennis analogy to emphasize why the best process alone, without guidance and support, cannot bring effective results.

> *If you put a tennis racket in the hands of a good player, he will play a pretty good game. But if you give that same racket to Andre Agassi, he will play an amazing game. Business as a whole has just focused on the racket. If you give the racket to a weak player, you will not get the results you want, and you can't blame the racket.*

If managers understand how the performance evaluation process links to overall business goals and they believe that senior leaders understand the sacrifices they make to comply with the process, HR will earn cooperation. With practice, the evaluation process will get easier, and, as line managers realize improved performance, HR will become a valued partner.

Include Development Planning

Providing development opportunities for all—the Positioning discussed in depth in Chapter Three, *Managing Inclusion*—is integral to a culture of development. It is also the cornerstone of effective performance management. HR's role in this process is to work with managers to help them succeed in their own development—learning the process and mastering the skills needed to use and develop all employees.

The first challenge for managers is to define individual development opportunities. This requires knowing each employee and his or her work well enough to assess the level of challenge that is appropriate for each. HR can provide managers with individual assessment guides to help them set challenging but realistic goals for the employees, along with creating individual development plans. Over time, the process will become second nature, but in the beginning managers need encouragement to practice these new managerial skills. HR is responsible for the review process that can provide managers with the structure and support necessary to ensure that each employee has challenging and realistic goals in place at the start of each year.

The second challenge managers have is making sure that each of their employees has the support needed to achieve the goals. This means guiding and coaching each employee as he or she tackles challenging work assignments, ensuring that he or she has the resources and cooperation from others to execute the plans, and ensuring that the steps and activities in the individual development plans are carried out. HR can support this process by monitoring progress throughout the year.

Managers already know the basic behaviors; they have always engaged in them for those identified as the talented few.

What is required is to extend those same benefits to everyone. The challenge is to unlock enthusiasm and ambition in everyone, to inspire their improved performance. There will be immediate improvement from many employees, but others will require perseverance. Again, a strategic HR can foster the environment that encourages perseverance while reinforcing the need to meet standards. With commitment from HR, the development process will become the new standard, "the way we do things."

Promote Constructive Feedback

A culture of development languishes as nothing more than a pipedream when employees do not receive constructive feedback from their managers, either during the annual review process or more informally throughout the year. Fear of providing that essential feedback is a major stumbling block for many managers, and we discussed in Chapter 3, *Managing Inclusion*, many strategies for overcoming this obstacle. Here we look critically at how HR can support managers in their efforts to master delivering the kind of feedback that leads to improved performance, the difficult-to-obtain information every employee needs in order to achieve success. Feedback is not necessarily positive or negative— it is equally helpful following both successes and failures—and it has nothing to do with feeling embarrassed or guilty.

It can be delivered formally during the annual performance evaluation, or it can be more of a running commentary or series of conversations. In fact, where feedback is woven into the daily fabric of business life, its impact is enhanced.

Providing feedback in the beginning is complex and fraught with risk and feelings of discomfort. What can and should HR be doing to ease the transition throughout an organization? Managers deserve HR guidance and training through this transition as they work to become proficient at delivering constructive feedback. Key features of any HR guidance and training would be:

- Feedback should focus on job-related behavior not personal tastes. "Your dress is too short (or shorts too casual) for this office" is valuable information, but "I don't like the way you look at me" or "Your desk is too messy looking" are probably not appropriate.
- Feedback should be interactive rather than a lecture. Targeted questions, for example, "What would have been a better way to handle that question you were not prepared for?" foster a better reception and outcome because they ask the employee to participate in the learning.
- Feedback should be about specific actions. Here are three examples of helpful feedback (helpful because the employee understands exactly what to do going forward).

> *You opened the meeting today by clarifying the exact purpose. That helped us stay on task and make good use of our time.*

> *The three typos in the proposal may have suggested to the client that our company doesn't value quality. If you proof your correspondence before sending it, your close rate may increase.*

> *When Fred told you that you made a mistake, maybe you should have asked, "How?" instead of arguing with him right off the bat.*

To understand the difference, consider these similar but un-helpful messages,

I couldn't tell what you were trying to do in that meeting.

Your written work is really sloppy.

You were defensive in there.

Equally difficult is having no feedback it all—silence. Em-ployees are left in the dark, with their assumptions and general impressions—"That seemed to go just fine"—or worse, the ter-rible feeling in your stomach that doesn't go away. Feedback, to be helpful, has to be a road map for future performance.

Feedback must be constructive, well intentioned and designed to guide an employee to improved performance. It is not a free pass at vengeance or spite and is no place for left-handed compliments. To tell someone, for example, "You always mess everything up," or "That was better than I ever expected from you," is feedback, but it makes a mockery of what we are talking about.

INTERNAL SOURCING—LATERAL TRANSFERS AND PROMOTIONS

Today, with flattened organizations increasingly the rule, HR knows that developing skills and experience cannot always lead to promotions. With diminishing opportunities for advancement, organizations are beginning to understand the value of lateral moves. Even in the absence of promotion, lateral Positioning can provide many new and satisfying work experiences which are also platforms for developing new skills. Open and rigorous internal sourcing, especially in the case of lateral transfers, is in fact a key strategy in a culture of development.

Internal sourcing is about Position—providing development opportunities to everyone, along with the managerial support and guidance to ensure success. Managers who can be convinced to look beyond the same old "go-to" people and Position all their staff will achieve greater productivity. It is in HR's interest to make this happen, to see that managers match business needs to the development opportunities they create.

Job postings are another corporate internal sourcing strategy that taps into the ambitions of current employees, yet the supposed openness of job postings is not living up to its promise. The results, visible to all, are not seen as being available to everyone. In focus group after focus group, employees express their belief that not all jobs are posted, and that the ones that are posted are defined either so narrowly that everyone knows a specific candidate has already been identified, or so broadly that no one can understand the qualifications.

When employees do interview for positions, many find the process "pro forma," and they have to struggle to get feedback about their shortcomings so they can plan for a more successful presentation in the future. Some employees don't get any feedback at all. One ambitious young manager we know described her unsuccessful efforts.

When I found out I had not been selected, I went to HR to ask why. I didn't want to complain; I wanted to improve

myself so I'd have a better chance at the next opportunity.
They told me nothing. I went to my manager, and he told
me nothing. I didn't know what else to do.

What is an employee to think in these circumstances? Was the rejection truly objective? Was the person selected the best choice for the company? Should she stop applying? Is it possible to improve, and if so, how? She will never know, and her lack of information can cause other problems as well. Those informational voids can easily get filled with wrong ideas, for example, that women and people of color have no real opportunity here. One HR executive warns:

In the absence of information, people are going to fill the
gap with all kinds of wild ideas. You can't let them do
that. Even information they may not want to hear is better
than no information.

The manager in our example was an African-American woman, so she might decide race and/or gender were deciding factors. An unsuccessful white man can be equally misled, especially if the successful candidate was a woman or person of color. He may very well blame the decision on reverse discrimination, and he, too, will have been effectively denied the opportunity to improve himself for the next application. Or worse, both of them may begin to disengage from their work. This is where strategic HR training and oversight can make a difference and actually promote a culture of development, altering the equation. HR can make sure that objective standards are used in internal sourcing, that the process is transparent, and that candidates receive accurate feedback.

How do women and people of color *fare* in internal sourcing? [buttermilk]
Do they have better results selling themselves in such situations?
Even with diminishing promotion opportunities for all, the disproportionate absence of women and people of color at higher
levels remains troubling. Achieving company-wide representation numbers is only Step One; numbers alone do not signal an
inclusive work environment. A Chief Diversity Officer explained
the challenge:

> *You can't breathe a sigh of relief because you have
> women and people of color in the pipeline. The real
> questions begin with, "Who is the next obvious choice
> and why?" You have to peel back the onion on what the
> actual qualifications are. What experiences—educational,
> operational, developmental, etc.—are really necessary?
> Do candidates really need them? If the answer is yes, did
> the women and people of color get them? Where do they
> fall short? Then we can accelerate women and people of
> color getting those experiences. You can never bypass
> the process because that only leads to the complaint that
> they are less qualified.*

How is that process working at his company? Although he
is now a key player in the succession planning process, he readily admits, "The jury is still out." As we have seen time and time
again, it requires a deliberate and conscious decision to include
women and people of color. Someone in a position to decide has
to say, "I'm going to make this happen."

An executive vice-president of HR stated the real goal of his
company's development initiatives this way:

*Ultimately, all the development activities we're involved
in have to lead to something. You want to get people
better prepared AND then get them to the next round.
We track promotions very carefully to make sure we don't
lose the diversity.*

No one is talking about putting people into a job to fulfill
a representation target. These companies have simply made the
necessary conscious decisions to include women and people of
color. If a company's commitment to the development of everyone is real, it won't be difficult to find diverse, qualified people.

With so much talent going to waste, why do so many companies fail to seize these obvious development opportunities? When
a wake-up call yields such excellent results, we wonder why any
company waits for a crisis. The Home Depot, for example, had
a reputation as a company that promoted from within. Without
any examination, they rested on those laurels. Women, however,
knew that they were not beneficiaries of that policy. Finally, a
group of women in the company's West Coast stores, mostly ca-
shiers, took the company to court. In response, The Home Depot
set up a company-wide computer system to handle all applications from potential and current employees. The system culled
all applicants for basic qualifications.

For every opening, each store manager had to access the
system, cut first for his or her own store and then geographic
district, and interview three applicants. According to the former
board member who oversaw the company-wide transformation:

*We made sure the managers gave feedback to internal
candidates who didn't get the job. Managers had to tell*

them how they did in the interview and what things they
could do to be more successful next time. Together, they
then wrote a development plan, which became a part of
our system.

At first, many managers were resistant, but they found they actually spent less time finding new employees this way than they had through their informal networks. Moreover, the new employees were better qualified, more enthusiastic, and fit into their jobs more quickly. Many of them were found right within their own stores. Most managers became strong supporters of the system, and those who did not comply, even if their stores were top performers, were replaced. In this case, a consent decree requiring a narrow change became the incentive for fostering real inclusion and a true culture of development.

Internal sourcing decisions that are transparent, are based on open and clear criteria, that require broad, diverse slates of candidates, and include constructive and timely feedback to those who are not selected, are key ingredients of a culture of development. A strategic HR department is in a position to change policy and practice, perception and reality, and improve performance across the company. We are not advocating risky behavior, because from every angle, an inclusive culture of development is in the best interest of the business. All that is needed is the will.

SUCCESSION PLANNING

Decisions about promotions to the highest levels, planned over a longer period of time, are collectively referred to as succession planning. Until recently, succession planning was the concern of a few board members, who saw it as additional protection for the shareholders' investment. Not enough companies took the hint, however. Laments one sales executive we work with:

> There's no backup plan, no cross training, no real succession planning, in corporate America today. Companies need to invest in what I call executive bullpens, like the Yankees, so they have people being developed while they are in holding patterns. They should be getting a chance to move across the country, across the company. What happens instead is somebody decides to move on or retires, and someone at the top says, "I need somebody who can hit the ground running. Who do I know?" They just move the same few people around and give them other titles.

Today, senior leadership has realized the value of succession planning for guiding companies through inevitable transitions like retirement, the voluntary or involuntary departure of top personnel, and other contingencies and emergencies. Bringing in new CEOs or other top officers from the outside has become almost prohibitively expensive, in part because bidding wars break out again and again over the same few people. Recent surveys suggest that the expense may not be worth it, because home-grown CEOs frequently outperform those brought in from the outside.

These experiences make building bench strength an even more compelling business strategy, and a serious commitment to succession planning meshes perfectly with the goals of a culture of development. One vice-president of Human Resources explained his conclusion this way:

The idea that great leaders are born so is way, way too risky to rely on. My view is you've got to build making great leaders into the culture. This means developing a rigorous process that says, "There are certain rites of passage you must go through, or you're not going on to the next level." It has to be a well laid-out process, with clear stages in people's careers, where we teach them our way of doing things. You need certain skills and experiences in your tool kits, from inclusion to great financial skill, a whole raft of skills you don't get in school. We've learned what works for us; these are the things we value. You need to be good at these things to have a successful career in this company.

In his company, succession planning embodies the components of a culture of development: clear standards for selection, both technical and behavioral competencies, a process for positioning people to receive the necessary development opportunities and experiences, and feedback about performance. When the process is open and transparent like this, people who are interested in advancement to the highest levels know what they have to do, and they can develop a strategy and a reasonable timetable for doing so. Bench strength is likely to be maximized.

Another company committed to an open process actually analyzed the career paths of those in the top positions, identifying a number of key positions that were traditionally a part of their work experiences. According to its Chief Diversity Officer,

We identified those "feeder jobs" in each business unit, and we're looking to recruit, develop and promote

women and people of color into those jobs. That's the only way they will be ready to move up eventually into senior management roles. We don't tell anyone to take a certain person, but just putting a spotlight on those jobs has helped.

It's too early to tell if the practice will yield a more diverse team of vice-presidents, but the odds have been significantly increased.

Can we assume that most companies understand the value of an open and objective succession planning process? Unfortunately not. Most companies, if they plan for succession at all, follow a process wrapped in secrecy. Only a select few executives know the names under consideration, the criteria for being selected, and the kinds of experiences and behavioral competencies they expect their future leaders to have. They justify the secret process by saying:

- they don't want to be held to implied promises;
- they don't want to lessen the energy of those who have been passed over; and
- they don't want those on the list to think they can rest on their laurels because their future success is secured.

Are these concerns valid? Some who know they were passed over may disengage, but most were probably not fully committed to the work anyway. And if those who learn they are on the list begin to slack off, they probably should never have been tapped for higher positions in the first place. As to the issue of an implied promise, the corporate legal department can readily supply suitable language. Upon examination, most of the stated reasons look like excuses to remain in control of the process. The results behind these closed doors are most likely going to be based on the default position of "some have it, and some don't," the original "Castes in Concrete," sort-and-select, subjective process that excludes most people. A strategic HR can advocate for the best interest of the business: a more open and objective process.

How do our canaries in the mine—women and people of color, as well as other disenfranchised groups—fare in the secret club environment? It will come as no surprise that they are seldom selected. Leaders who aren't asked to meet objective criteria are most likely to choose people who seem "just like me." Further, where the process is not transparent, even a leader who decides to advocate on behalf of a woman or person of color can receive derogatory push-back from his colleagues: "Why is she so special to you?" or "Is this your personal affirmative action program at work?" For change to occur, a leader has to stand firm in the face of innuendo, sarcasm and other indications of resistance to change.

Even in the most closely guarded succession planning processes, a few diverse candidates get tapped. What happens to them? They tend to fall into the "ready in three to five years" category, and three to five years later they are still in that category. Without managers, mentors, coaches or supporters, they are at sea. No one informs them of their high-potential status, articulates the criteria for advancement, sets them on a path to developing the necessary qualifications, skills and experiences, or then advocates for their selection. A more open process would begin to change those results, and HR can lead the way.

Most companies realize their future success depends on a more inclusive succession planning process, and they are looking for ways to equalize opportunity. Women represent roughly one-half the population the world over, and in countries outside Europe and North America, companies are virtually all what we in the west refer to euphemistically as diverse. Even in Europe and North America, the population and the labor pool are becoming increasingly diverse. This aspect of our future is not unknowable.

To transform almost every interaction at work is a complex and slow process; nothing takes more time, patience and diplomacy to accomplish than behavior change. A strategic HR is in the best position to guide the process of changing "our normal way of doing business" as well as to alter the tenor of internal discussions about an inclusive culture of development. Companies on the path have all relied on HR leadership. In the next chapter, we look at structural changes that, working in concert with a strategic HR, can jump-start progress toward a culture of development.

CHAPTER SIX

Jump-starting Inclusion

Establishing the Infrastructure

If you're in the room, there are teachable moments.

Robert Spencer
Chief Inclusion Officer
Entergy

Building an inclusive culture of development is everyone's job. At the same time, we also know that any major organizational initiative designed to bring about change requires an infrastructure with clearly defined roles and responsibilities, and with accountability to ensure that what people have committed to do will, in fact, happen. In this chapter we examine some common structures that organizations have put in place to help direct and support their inclusion and development efforts. In most cases these companies use the term "diversity"—for example, "Senior Diversity Officer." Given our definition of diversity and inclusion, we recommend using the term "inclusion" because it describes the true goal—an inclusive culture of development.

THE SENIOR INCLUSION OFFICER

In Chapter Four, *Strategic Leadership*, we talked about the critical role senior leaders play in moving an organization from compliance to internalization on issues of culture change, such as moving toward an inclusive culture of development. But senior leaders have to balance their inclusion and development activities with many other responsibilities. We have found the organizations that are most successful in achieving their inclusion and development goals are often those with a senior person dedicated to making inclusion and a culture of development a reality. That senior leader is typically referred to as the Senior Inclusion Officer (SIO), Chief Diversity Officer (CDO) or VP or Director of Diversity or Inclusion. Given the synergy between inclusion and leadership development, that officer's duties ideally either cover training and development or coordinate with those functions through a dotted-line relationship.

We hope and expect that in the not-too-distant future there will be no need for such a person, because the value of an inclusive workplace—where everyone is truly committed to developing the talent of all—will be an integral part of corporate culture. In the meantime, companies experiment with where that person sits in the organizational chart. Any position has advantages and disadvantages, and each company has to decide what will work best in its particular environment.

We strongly recommend that, regardless of where the position is located, it carry the weight and authority to influence the key decisions needed to integrate inclusion throughout the organization. In our experience this is most likely to happen when the Senior Inclusion Officer heads a stand-alone department and reports directly to the CEO. For that reason we begin our discussion with that arrangement, and then examine the benefits and limitations of other common approaches.

Stand-alone Department

Until inclusion and a culture of development are permanently embedded in every aspect of corporate life, practitioners are nearly unanimous in their belief that the optimum strategy is a stand-alone department, headed by a vice-president who reports to the board chair or vice-chair, a board committee or the full board, CEO and/or COO. This conclusion is almost inevitable once the premise of investing in a company's human capital is understood as crucial to future business success. The key factor in this reporting structure is the SIO's seat at the table where decisions are made.

All senior executives know the value of that seat, and change begins to accelerate when skilled inclusion professionals have access to it. One SIO told us why this access to the decision-makers led her to prefer her company's executive committee to a seat on the board.

> The discussion at first was I would have a seat on the board. I told my chairman I wanted a seat on the management committee. If I sat on the board, I'd be hearing decisions already made, and I'd be in the position of having to remake them. I want to influence decisions. One of the positive results is I hear my words coming out

of other people's mouths. For example, in one meeting we were putting up names for a sales position. Before I could open my mouth to say anything, the vice-chairman said, "Where are the women?" That felt great.

A seat at the table is an opportunity to bring insight to other leaders. Here's how a different SIO described his view of the opportunity.

When you have a seat at the table, you can be that coach, that counselor. There'll occasionally be a decision that they're not even aware of the impact. If you're there, you can say, "Do you realize what we just did?"

For a third inclusion officer, the advantages go beyond personnel decisions.

Now I get unfiltered information. I hear the business challenges firsthand, so I can channel my quality treatment messages to fit the business challenges. That makes it easier for everyone to understand the business case.

That kind of access signals that leadership is serious about results and may entice respected line officers to take on the inclusion challenge. One senior inclusion officer who had been in sales agreed to take the inclusion position only after it was restructured to report to the president.

We'd had diversity [and inclusion] leaders before, but they were mainly figureheads. This time, when they decided to appoint a line manager who understood the business and who would be a member of the executive team, it was a signal that they were serious about making progress. The people I would need to influence, who would actually have to deploy the strategy, knew and respected me. I didn't know how much of a difference I could make, but I could tell the structure was setting me up for success. And it did. Big-time.

With the support of the president of the organization, I was able to exceed where we thought we'd be now in terms of systemic change. That genie is clearly out of the bottle and will stay out. Inclusion is no longer an "aside" or a "program of the day." The company is totally aware of it, and people are going to keep asking about it, wanting to be a part of it and to keep it going.

In Human Resources

There are good reasons to consider other locations for the inclusion officer. Placement within a strategic HR, for example, can be effective if the issues are championed by the head of the department, and especially if that leader is also a senior executive and a significant policy player at the company.

One head of HR is such a player, and he knows how to manage inclusion as a business issue.

I'm fed up with the people who say, well, the inclusion thing happens over there. If we're going to build diversity and inclusion into the fabric of the business, then I want some senior person on my staff that reports directly to me, not three levels down, to be in charge of it.

If, however, the position is buried beneath layers of reporting, one of many competing human resources interests or requirements, results will be difficult to achieve.

Dotted-line relationships can increase the potential effectiveness of the inclusion officer's role as well. In one company, the inclusion officer reports to the executive vice-president of HR, but also reports twice a year to a board committee. The current SIO explains the advantages.

> *Just the fact that the board, with very tight agendas, wants to hear from me, means they're on top of the issue. The woman who chairs that committee is very outspoken, especially around inclusion and women's initiatives. The board therefore is very interested in inclusion. They ask a lot of questions. They push back.*

The board's interest makes the senior leadership team pay attention. That active oversight by the board commands the attention of the senior leadership team, no matter where the inclusion officer resides in the organizational chart.

In Legal

Placing the senior diversity and inclusion officer in Legal draws extreme opinions. Given the historical evolution of both diversity and inclusion, it may be difficult to separate current initiatives in people's minds from some negative connotations—governmental reporting requirements, compliance, affirmative action, EEO complaints and class action discrimination suits. One former board member of a Fortune 500 company explains why she so strongly opposes this placement.

Legal is the worst place for it to be. I understand why Legal would like to control it, because it is an area where they have tremendous fear. And precisely because of that fear, they don't stand a chance of understanding the concepts necessary to achieve real inclusion. If I were a cynical person, I'd say their defensiveness is in part because law firms and legal departments in large corporations are bad role models for inclusion. Inclusion and development are operating issues: issues of balance, hiring the best people, developing them and keeping them, creating a work environment where people can excel. You can't manage those issues from a legal department.

The confusion between Legal's traditional defensive posture and the expansive role of inclusion is unfortunate, since Legal's position is beginning to change. Today, more and more general counsels are playing a significant role on executive committees, being asked to head other departments, and even being groomed for the CEO slot. In such a setting, with a committed general counsel, the dedicated SIO could have significant clout.

In Strategic Planning

Some companies have experimented with placing the dedicated inclusion officer in strategic planning. While this sends a message that inclusion and development are considered critical to the business, those issues can also become buried among a number of competing and compelling interests.

One SIO finds that reporting structure makes sense for his company.

Our CEO and his direct reports believe inclusion and development are strategic issues for the company's growth over the next few years. Our recent growth has been through mergers. Now we have to grow from within, finding ways to make shrinking resources lead to higher output. We need to attract the best talent and then develop them so they will stay. Also, because of the level of criticism about large global corporations, it is not enough for us to say we don't have a problem. We need to show positive results. Putting diversity and inclusion in strategic planning sends the right message for our company.

There is no single universal right answer. Success depends in each case on the specific corporate culture, the sophistication of the practitioner and the level of senior executive support for the initiative. The bottom line is that each company must decide for itself what reporting structure makes the most sense. Look at your corporate culture, the make-up of your leadership team, and your organizational structure. A key question to ask is, "Where will the inclusion officer have the most visibility and credibility, as well as authority and influence over decisions related to inclusion and development?

THE EXECUTIVE STEERING COMMITTEE

Another inclusion strategy that works in harmony with an SIO is an Executive Steering Committee whose members are department heads and senior leaders and which is chaired by the CEO. We find the most effective committees have the mission of developing a company-specific business case for building an inclusive culture of development, examining relevant data and creating a strategic plan that is integrated into the overall business strategy. In some organizations, Executive Steering Committees disband once the rest of the inclusion infrastructure is in place. In others, they remain active as an opportunity for ongoing executive leadership and support.

One company has established an Inclusion Leadership Team headed by the company president, and its twelve members include the vice-presidents of operations, compliance, HR and marketing, the directors of the business units, and a team leader from the technical ranks. They meet quarterly, and the senior inclusion officer, although he reports to the vice-president of HR, meets regularly with the CEO to give him updates.

A company president told us about his own change of heart, brought about by his position as head of his company's Steering Committee, which over the years evolved into an important contributor to business strategy:

> *Our approach is now systemic and long-lasting, and there's much more buy-in. You have to do a lot of work to get past the guilt and avoidance, but I think that's the nature of social change.*

This leader's own personal journey explains part of the reason this organization's current Inclusion Committee is so successful.

> *Twenty years ago diversity and inclusion felt too much like taking your cod liver oil every day. Now it's really fun. People are enthusiastic, positive, contributing,*

volunteering. Life is richer. I'm a believer that inclusion is
not for the benefit of what used to be called the protected
groups but for the benefit of the entire organization.

Figure 6.1, Creating an Effective Executive Steering Committee, summarizes our recommendations based on years of experience with many companies. With these guidelines, your Executive
Steering Committee is most likely to be a successful part of the
infrastructure for an inclusive culture of development.

Figure 6.1: Creating an Effective Executive Steering Committee

	Considerations for an Effective Steering Committee
Mission/ Objectives	Focus the mission/objectives on providing executive leadership and direction to the inclusion initiative, especially in its early stages. This includes: 1) clearly articulating the business case, 2) integrating inclusion and development into the business strategy and goals, 3) supporting other inclusion-related structures (e.g., inclusion councils and affinity groups).
Leadership Selection	Select the leader based on commitment and time available as well as inclusion-related knowledge and experience. In some cases, the senior-most member will assume the role of the leader. Ideally, the leader will be an executive who has internalized the values of inclusion and development and has the ability to inspire others to do likewise.

Philosophy	Emphasize the leadership role of the steering committee in terms of providing guidance and ensuring that inclusion and development become integrated into the business philosophy and strategy. Members should also view themselves as "role models" when they interact with others in the organization.
Structure	Optimize effectiveness by size ranging from 8 to 15 members. The majority should come from the executive ranks. Guard against the tendency to be strictly hierarchical by providing the mechanisms so that all members, including non-executives, actively participate.
Executive Support	Demonstrate executive support by actively serving on the steering committee and by allocating resources.
Visibility	Articulate the importance of inclusion and development, both verbally and through concrete action. Include these topics in formal presentations and communications as an integral part of the business strategy. Openly communicate the activities and decisions of the steering committee throughout the organization.
Membership Eligibility	Select at least half the members from line and staff officers of the company. Include one or more members of the operating/executive committee. Non-executive employees can be invited to participate so that women and people of color are included—to improve the quality of the input and provide credibility for the outcomes.

Continued

Quality of Involvement	Establish specific, goal-oriented agenda items for each meeting. Require regular attendance at meetings and active involvement in the work of the group. Determine the frequency of meetings by the nature of the objectives to be met.
Funding	Share the investment in time and expense: business-related and public-relations activities sponsored by the company; volunteer efforts shared; social events sponsored by the membership.

EMPLOYEE-BASED INCLUSION COUNCILS

While leadership commitment, as evidenced, for example, by an Executive Steering Committee, is crucial, a complementary strategy for engaging a broader band of employees is an Inclusion Council. Inclusion Council membership covers a wide range of levels and functional groups as well as key diversity categories, a selection process often referred to as a "diagonal" or "Z" slice of the organization. Large companies adapt the strategy to multiple locations and business units by establishing a series of Inclusion Councils, perhaps one in each location or one for each Business Unit. The network of councils then reports to the Executive Steering Committee, which coordinates the network's information and recommendations to decide how best to further the company's inclusion and development goals. As such, they are a critical link between the employee population and senior leaders.

The Executive Steering Committee and/or Senior Diversity Office may also delegate certain responsibilities to the Diversity Councils—for example, asking them to conduct research and make specific recommendations on the types of skill-building that managers need. A secondary advantage of these Councils is their ability to model inclusion by their very existence.

To form Inclusion Councils, companies have experimented with a variety of structures and processes, for example, using volunteer members with no formal connection to the leadership or business strategy, or employee-driven bodies. Some of these voluntary councils have made important contributions, such as raising employee awareness about the value of diversity and inclusion. But many such councils have proved ineffective, or they have floundered and even been disbanded. Many of their problems actually stemmed from their volunteerism, because members felt free to use them as opportunities to vent or complain. A client described his disappointment as a member of one such council.

> *It was like a mini–United Nations, and not in the good sense. Everybody had volunteered to make sure that "my group" got heard—everybody had a different agenda and nothing got accomplished.*

Another limiting factor was their lack of a formal relationship with senior leaders. Because they were not connected to a committed, invested executive who served as a member or sponsor of the council, their activities may have been educational and fun but had little to do with harnessing inclusion to benefit the business.

To be most effective, therefore, we recommend Inclusion Councils have a clear mission that describes how their work will align inclusion with a company's business. Further, membership should be based on selection criteria rather than volunteering.

One major energy company's experience with Inclusion Councils is a good example of the benefits that can accrue over time when a company builds understanding of their value. Begun with a series of independent councils throughout the company, each led by lower-level employees, they evolved into a formal reporting relationship, via a steering committee, with the leadership team. The company's senior inclusion officer explained part of his role as liaison.

> *I certainly convey a corporate perspective to the seventeen councils, and I get important communication back from them. Since I report to the CEO, their concerns and recommendations become part of his agenda.*

As many companies have also discovered, selecting employees from a diagonal or Z slice of the organization to serve on Inclusion Councils has an additional advantage. It provides another opportunity to identify promising employees they might not otherwise have noticed.

The chart in Figure 6.2 summarizes our recommendations, based on our years of experience in many companies, for forming and maintaining successful Inclusion Councils.

Figure 6.2: Forming and Maintaining Effective Inclusion Councils

	Considerations for an Effective Inclusion Council
Mission/ Objectives	Support inclusion by gathering information, making recommendations to the Steering Committee and participating in implementation. Clearly articulate the degree of responsibility/decision-making authority that the Inclusion Council has over specific areas. Define the relationship between the inclusion council and other groups, for example, an executive-level steering committee or affinity groups.
Leadership Selection	Select leaders based on their: • demonstrated capacity to focus on the greater good of the whole enterprise • records of value-added job performance over time • reputation (across levels and diverse groups) for objectivity, fairness and basic good judgment • excellent verbal and written communication skills
Philosophy	Emphasize the dual role of the council—both providing information, support and recommendations, as well as constituting a concrete demonstration of diversity and inclusion in action. Members should view themselves as "role models" in their daily interactions.

Continued

Structure	Select a "diagonal slice" of the organization, including members from diverse groups. This is essential to establish credibility and broad organizational support for council activities. Establish a reporting relationship to the Steering Committee (or other executive group) to ensure that the council's activities are in alignment with the company's core business strategies and goals.
Executive Support	Provide the council with sponsorship, time and resources. Participate in council-sponsored activities. Take council recommendations seriously and provide prompt feedback and, when appropriate, approval.
Visibility	Create mechanisms to communicate council activities to the organization, for example, by sponsoring an inclusion newsletter or "brown bag" lunches during which specific issues are discussed.
Membership Eligibility	Select members based on specific criteria consistent with inclusion and development. Establish a system for rotating membership so that a percentage of the council will turn over each year.
Quality of Involvement	Develop specific, goal-oriented agenda items for each meeting. Require regular attendance at meetings and active involvement in the work of the group. Determine the frequency of meetings by the nature of the objectives to be met.

Funding	Establish a budget for the Inclusion Council. When considerable time is expected of council members, consider ways to include this role as part of their job responsibility with a percentage of time (e.g., 10%) allocated for council activitites.

AFFINITY GROUPS

In general, affinity groups, or employee networks, are groups of people who share common diversity or job-related characteristics. These groups serve many different functions, depending on the goals of the particular members and their relationship to the company leadership. Most groups share common cultural, experiential or functional bonds; for example, members may all be African-Americans, Latinos, women, gays and lesbians, salaried workers or engineers.

The first affinity groups were established by African-Americans because they felt isolated and sought solace among other, similarly isolated employees. Initially, a number of those early groups felt it necessary to meet outside company time and off location. Over several decades, though, these and other affinity groups have evolved into company-supported organizations that support both career development for members and company business goals.

One head of HR we work with uses his own personal experience to advocate for support for affinity groups within his company.

I remember distinctly being an eastern Jew at one company years ago. I was one of five—out of 90,000 employees. I used to describe myself as a sojourner, somehow in a foreign land. When I met with one other Jew who worked near me, we didn't know it, but we were the affinity group!

So I see their value. They give people a sense of solace, of safety, of belonging. "I'm just not comfortable in this world, and if I can have a few moments together with folks who feel like I do, I can get a lot more comfortable a lot faster. I could also learn from the others about how to get around, how to work the system." That's good for the company, so I'm a big fan of them.

In addition to providing mutual support, many affinity groups now provide direct help to the organization in internal and external recruiting. At one company's affinity group, members refer people to the company for openings, and they staff company booths at job fairs. As the senior diversity officer explained it,

They're out there on the front line, talking to people about opportunities here. We also tap members as buddies when we're trying to recruit someone. We'll ask a member to take that person out to dinner. Meeting someone "like them" for dinner, out of the building, in a relaxed situation, they can answer a lot of questions. That's been helpful to us.

There are also many examples of affinity groups helping to retain valued employees. One sales executive described how his department benefited.

We know of a lot of people who would have left if it weren't for the network, especially women and minorities in remote locations. It's not that the company is a bad place to work, but people go through episodes, like a communication problem with a manager or a boss. The group has been able to save them. That's a great value for us.

A newer development is using affinity groups for more direct business assistance, such as providing an important sounding board for a new product or improved service. These groups become a sort of in-house marketing focus group. This is one of the most direct examples of how a more diverse workforce can lead companies to tap effectively into new and broader markets.

The networks are a great way to say, "How does that sound to you? What should we be thinking about?" I can't think of anything worse for our business than a bunch of white males sitting around the room trying to figure out what they want. As much as I could intellectually walk in someone else's shoes, I couldn't quite get all the way there. So we've been working with a cross-section of the networks in a more formal way to bounce off ideas. It takes time to build trust, for the groups to believe we really want their opinion, not just their surface approval. Now we sometimes hear things we don't want to hear. They're not shrinking violets!

In one large company, a networking group acted as a focus group when the organization was getting ready to start a marketing push into new territory.

We asked them to come in and represent the Latino community, as if they were no longer an employee here, to help us understand how to engage the culture of this area. We got great information our marketing team used in designing the rollout. We certainly gave them a lot of recognition inside the company. We made sure people knew that's the kind of thing that can happen when employees come together and give of themselves.

The fact that, in some ways, affinity groups separate themselves from the organization does not have to be a problem, and companies address the issue in different ways. One senior inclusion officer gave us this example.

In our company we require that our network groups be open to any employee; anybody at any level can participate. We also ask them to do projects that everyone can support, and so skill development has become the focus. Everybody benefits from that.

If the separation is seen as a necessary step toward fitting in—a step that helps members gather their strength and gain a sense of individual empowerment—then it is ultimately a benefit to the organizational goal.

If people have the informal support that comes from the group, they are better able to manage their careers. That's good for us because in the end they feel more connected to the firm.

As with Executive Steering Committees and Inclusion Councils, Affinity Groups can be more effective if their goals, membership and activities are carefully planned and linked to the business goals of the wider organization. While companies will differ in the specifics of their strategies, we recommend you consider the following guidelines when supporting the formation of affinity groups (see Figure 6.3).

Figure 6.3: Supporting Effective Affinity Groups

	Considerations for an Effective Affinity Group
Mission/ Objectives	Develop a short, straightforward, business-oriented statement about why the group exists. State every goal in terms that clearly serve both the membership and the company. Update goals annually to take into account the changing needs of the people and the organization.
Leadership Selection	Elect leaders based on their: • demonstrated capacity to focus on the greater good of the whole enterprise • records of value-added job performance over time • reputations (across levels and diverse groups) for objectivity, fairness and basic good judgment • excellent verbal and written communication skills

Continued

Philosophy	Adopt a "no-blame"/"nothing to hide" orientation to under-gird the group's strategies and activities. This philosophy requires a commitment from both the membership and the corporation to take full responsibility for finding mutually beneficial solutions to issues of importance.
Structure	Ensure cross-functional and cross-level membership. Build group consensus for critical decision-making. Be explicit about the expectation of hard work in support of the mission. Show no tolerance for personal agendas.
Executive Support	Seek the backing of the CEO and his/her direct reports for the philosophy and goals of the group. Schedule regular meetings with key stakeholders not only to keep them apprised of the work of the group, but also to keep the group apprised of the core issues of the business.
Visibility *	Voluntarily share information about major initiatives, concerns and recommendations. Publish group results. Demonstrate support for other affinity group efforts. Become active participants in program initiatives of the business (e.g., new-product launches, achieving safety goals).
Membership Eligibility *	Make membership 100% voluntary. Make eligibility to join/attend meetings non-exclusive to the affinity group, though the agenda can and should remain targeted.

Quality of Involvement	Establish specific, goal-oriented agenda items for each meeting. Require regular attendance at meetings and active involvement in the work of the group. Determine the frequency of meetings by the nature of the objectives to be met.
Funding *	Share the investment in time and expense: business-related and public-relations activities sponsored by the company; volunteer efforts shared; social events sponsored by the membership.

* Optional considerations are highly recommended because of the probable problems they solve. They are optional because of their controversial nature and the requirement that the group itself manage that controversy.

MENTORING PROGRAMS

What is a mentor? The term has come to be shorthand for a long-term relationship with a person who provides advice and support that will make or break a career. Because so much hangs on the person wearing that label, it makes sense to think carefully about what mentors can realistically be expected to do. Disappointments arise because protégés are so hungry, even desperate, for that kind of wisdom. How can any one person satisfy so many needs? One person cannot.

In general, mentors are seasoned professionals who share wisdom with bright and energetic young people, what we call protégés. Mentors thus help shape protégés' potential into productivity by demonstrating work processes, sharing values, making introductions and providing advice. One young woman manager articulates perfectly how a mentor helped her to understand an unwritten rule about appropriate behavior during meetings:

> *I would watch people in a meeting stumbling over each other trying to get a word in just because the boss was at the head of the table, and I didn't want to be that way. I never wanted to fight anyone or do anything obnoxious. I thought I didn't need to talk all the time for people to know that I had something valuable to say. Big mistake! They assumed I said nothing because I had nothing to say. They decided I had no value. But until I got some mentoring, I could never understand why I was left out.*

What is obvious to some people almost on instinct was not obvious to her. In fact, she considered the "appropriate" behavior bad behavior. In some circumstances, her belief would have been correct, but not in the give-and-take among ambitious and engaged young managers. Someone had to tell her she had to join in the competition to be noticed—or valued.

Traditional Informal Mentoring

We start by defining mentor in more realistic terms. By mentor we mean an influential person who supports the development of the protégé's business acumen and professional maturity by helping him or her understand and manage the more subjective aspects of professional life.

Sometimes successful people can be surprisingly quick to say they never had a mentor. But we have found what they really mean is that they never had only one such person; they found and developed many supportive relationships along the way, all of whom could be thought of as mentors. Those who are successful in corporations have all had the benefit of support from wise, seasoned professionals, people in a position to advance their careers. Sometimes it was an unexpected word of encouragement, sometimes it came on one specific project, sometimes it lasted over a period of time, and sometimes it came from someone you didn't even know was following your career. In short, potential allies appear in as many different relationships as human beings can imagine—long-term, short-term, sporadic, constant, easy, difficult, intense, and distant—and they can be found at any level and at any time in any organization.

Until recently, that support most often came informally, through relationships bonded by personal identification: experiential, familial, social set or school networks. As the pool of new recruits has broadened, however, many more employees have arrived without a link to the traditional bonding networks. Certainly some were able to build solid and career-advancing relationships with company leaders, but most were in the dark, not even understanding the importance of those relationships, let alone how to establish them. Company leaders were equally in the dark about building links to those with whom they felt little or no personal identification.

Why a Formal Mentoring Program?

We recommend that companies establish formal mentoring programs to jump-start supportive relationships where the bonds of personal identification are not so obvious. While such programs will never replace the effectiveness of relationships that grow

naturally, they can break the ice for many, both mentors and protégés, and give each the courage to go on to form bonds more
naturally throughout the company. If the formalized relationship
actually becomes long-lasting, giving personal and professional
satisfaction to both mentor and protégé, so much the better. And
it is worth noting that such programs are cost effective, requiring
a relatively small number of hours of consultant time to design
the program according to company goals, train mentors and protégés, assess program operation periodically and modify as appropriate and then evaluate the program's overall effectiveness.

What should a formal program look like? Should it cover all
new hires? Every professional? Or should it just focus on those
identified for leadership positions or those above a certain level?
Should it be offered only to women and people of color? To everyone? Should mentoring be a required behavioral competency,
a factor in promotion decisions for the mentors? There is no
single right answer, and many different approaches have yielded
valuable returns.

A major consumer products company focuses its formal
mentoring program on succession candidates of color. Program
participants are identified when they reach middle management,
usually after three to five years of experience. According to this
recently retired SIO,

> We weren't getting the promotion batting average we
> wanted for employees of color, and their turnover was
> too high. So we structured a mentoring process for them,
> where they are matched with someone two levels above
> them, which means the mentor has about ten to fifteen
> years of experience. The candidates are getting far more

perspective and a more intense development experience, and we started to see better promotion and retention rates.

This narrow approach works for this company because it is helping achieve its overall inclusion goal. Programs at other companies approach the issue with a wide variety of techniques, and each of them has advantages and disadvantages. For example, programs which are open to all employees can become unwieldy or produce more protégés than mentors, leaving some disappointed. But such programs have the advantage of neutralizing backlash from employees who might feel excluded by more targeted programs. Programs at other companies hit every point along the spectrum between these two points. Those with effective programs do find better retention among the affected groups, and it is not unusual for more promotions to occur.

Creativity can usually find a way around every challenge. For example, where there are not enough managers willing and able to be formal mentors, group mentoring sessions give everyone a chance at a mentorship experience. For some, the group experience may be the best starting point; they have the opportunity to "wet their feet" in a less intense environment. One manager and several protégés learn from the mentor as well as from each other. In other companies, an innovative approach to mentoring has included "reverse mentoring," where leaders gain new insights from the perspective of younger employees. One well-known company used this approach to get its leaders up to speed technologically.

There is no one "right way" to structure a formal mentoring program. Your industry, the size of your company, your budget and time priorities, your company's geographical distribution and your particular business goals are all factors in determining the right program design for your company. As long as expectations are realistic and the program is part of an overall effort to build an inclusive culture of development, any carefully thought-out and well-planned program can succeed.

As with any new initiative, there will be a need to make adjustments along the way to incorporate new learning, and mentoring programs are no different. Many people can and do point to the problems and argue that the entire effort should be discontinued. We have found that most problems arise from inadequate guidance on the structure of the mentoring relationship, especially the failure to define roles and reasonable expectations for both mentors and protégés clearly and up-front. With this in mind, we have developed the following guidelines to help you plan and implement a successful mentoring program, regardless of who participates.

Guidelines for an Effective Mentoring Program

- Clarify the purpose of the mentoring relationship.
- Use objective criteria related to inclusion and development to select mentors and protégés.
- Clearly define the roles and responsibilities for both mentors and protégés. Make sure mentors are aware of and able to keep the time commitments.
- Provide mentors with the skills they need to be effective. Mentorship is one aspect of leadership, so developing mentors is an excellent example of how a culture of development actually benefits the entire organization.

- Be deliberate in pairing mentors and protégés. When feasible, involve participants in selecting their partners. After a few months, if the chemistry isn't working, offer opportunities to select new mentors and/or protégés.
- Initially plan for mentors and protégés to meet once a week. When relationships have been established, meetings can be less frequent but probably should take place at least once a month.
- Make protégés responsible for scheduling meetings and setting the agenda. This ensures that protégés will have an opportunity to take initiative, ensure that their concerns are addressed and balance the responsibility for the discussion among the pair.
- Provide sample topics for the first few meetings.
- Check in with participants regularly and use their feedback to make appropriate modifications to the program.

Over time and with shared experiences, both mentors and protégés will become more comfortable with each other, as familiarity and trust develop. In addition, protégés who have a positive mentoring experience will likely be more willing and able to serve as effective mentors to the next generation—including people who are different from them. As the process of mentoring expands beyond its traditional boundaries, the organization will have come a long way toward building a work environment that maximizes the potential of all. That's as good as it gets.

The strategies described in this chapter have been employed by many companies to further their inclusion and development goals and to align inclusion and development with the company's business purpose. But there is probably no limit to the number of effective strategies. Start with the experience of these companies, define your goals and then set your most creative minds to work.

CHAPTER SEVEN

Inclusion In The Global Economy

When assessing new people, places and challenges, it is imperative to cleanse the mind of any preconceived notions and ideas.

Carlos Ghosn
CEO, Nissan

Little more than two decades ago, "the global economy" was for most business leaders a topic of conversation rather than an operational reality. Very few companies were venturing outside their own borders, and those that did were primarily American and European companies doing business in each other's yards. Now the global economy is a fact of everyone's life.

• Mergers and acquisitions across borders are commonplace, and increasingly from East to West instead of West to East.

Asia Pacific Economic Cooperation (APEC)–developed economies account for about one-half of the close to $500 billion
worth of cross-border M&As, and the role of APEC developing economies has been increasing since the late 1990s. In almost every country, foreign companies are investing directly
and/or setting up subsidiaries, joint ventures and other forms
of business associations to conduct business.

- The Internet—expected to serve 1,000,000,000 users in 2005,
  tripled the number of users just five years earlier—and other
  technological advances have made global business communication instant. To say they are facilitating the conduct of business globally and in real time is an understatement.
- When trade barriers move up or down in any country, there
  are immediate global business consequences. Witness how:

  > oil prices rise as China's consumption surges; *(arıdan yükselme)*
  > steel prices rise as India's production grows;
  > China adjusts its apparel production schedules in response
    to Western quotas; or
  > EU retailers demanded increased quotas when the
    2005 quota on many Chinese apparel imports—valued at
    $8,000,000,000—was reached only halfway through the
    year, almost matching all Chinese apparel imports for
    2004.

- Porous borders throughout Europe, as well as immigration
  and emigration, are changing the composition of every workforce: *(içeriden dışarıya göç)*

  > 56 million migrants live in Europe;
  > 50 million migrants live in Asia; and
  > 41 million migrants live in North America.

These migrants represent 10 per cent of those living in developed economies, and their remittances to family members at home account for more than 10 per cent of GDP in nine of their own developing economies.

The way business is conducted and the way people live their work lives is being transformed. With so many people in developing economies preparing themselves and their children to participate in this global economy, the transformation will continue, often taking paths we cannot predict or foresee. The workforce in more and more countries will comprise an increasingly broad array of people representing different cultures, different perspectives and different experiences. While those differences offer the potential for new sources of creativity and unique contributions to the business, they also present the potential for miscommunication, inappropriate and inaccurate judgments and underutilization of the people resources we need to look to for business performance that gives a corporation a competitive edge. The concepts which underlie Positioning people for development, eliminating sources of Negative Treatment and providing Quality Treatment can facilitate an inclusive environment that fosters maximizing the performance of every employee and the organization overall. (See Chapters Two and Three for an in-depth discussion of these concepts.) We know that the definitions we have developed for Western cultures will not necessarily apply in every culture, but we also know that the basic concepts are relevant. The challenge in each culture is to acknowledge the conditions that permit or allow Negative Treatment and then to discover what Quality Treatment means there, i.e., what would inspire every employee to maximize his or her contribution to organizational goals in that particular cultural context.

Singapore and Malaysia, for example, experience a similar exclusionary practice that does not occur in the West but that few Westerners would have trouble understanding. In Singapore, where professionals from many countries come and work together in harmony, native Malays, as opposed to Chinese-Malay citizens, are often excluded. At one company we heard people say that Malays would not be hired, even if they were educated at a prestigious university and had worked successfully at other companies because they were perceived as "culturally lazy."

At another company in Malaysia, though, we heard about the twenty-year government experiment with affirmative action to encourage the hiring of native Malays. These discussions are familiar to U.S. managers, who have spent forty years working to eliminate similar perceptions about black Americans. It is an opportunity to share experiences and learnings, especially since the mistakes we have made are relatively well known abroad. We are all engaged in a process, and the "look" of talent will change, even if slowly, as it does in any healthy and growing culture.

In every completed cross-border business transaction, financial and legal due diligence was no doubt extensive. Lawyers, chartered accountants and business teams analyzed the strategic reason for the venture, the legal considerations and the timetable for realizing cost-saving synergies. What will the new market position be? How will it improve the company's competitive advantage? The analyses are challenging but the answers are quantifiable. Even so, results have not been easy to achieve. In cross-border M&As, indeed in at-home M&As, too many have found the projections to be inaccurate. Are cross-border transactions too complicated to be successful? The only possible answer is no; we simply have to learn from past mistakes and improve the procedure the next time.

How can the procedure be improved? We believe companies would realize better results and on an earlier timetable if they added new factors to their due diligence analysis, specifically the practices underlying inclusion and a culture of development.

- How do you integrate two businesses from different cultures?
- How do you allay the very natural fear and stress of the new situation, compounded by the unknowns of dealing with bosses from a completely different culture?
- How do you get people who are uncomfortable with, or even fearful of, different cultures to work together?
- How does anyone learn to communicate across the cultural divides in this dynamic new work environment?
- How can you prepare employees at every level to understand these cultural differences and then to work and live within them?

Although our global practice does not yet include follow-up over a period of years, our initial experiences have convinced us that all companies across the world would realize business benefits if they planned for inclusion, learned to understand their own exclusionary assumptions, and then overcame them in a proactive culture of development. The concepts of Negative Treatment, Quality Treatment, Position and Disposition, discussed in Chapters Two and Three, are effective bases for opening minds to new possibilities of improved performance and greater productivity.

MAKE THE BUSINESS CASE

When we work with clients preparing to enter a new global market or already in that market, we start with the business case for inclusion and a culture of development. How does a company draw the specific map of the business case in each new location? How can it best position itself to build cross-cultural bridges that lead to good working relationships? Here is a process we have found to be successful.

1. **Focus on full utilization of the workforce's capability.** This opening step brings into the operational context the basic premise of Quality Treatment: the belief that every employee has the capacity to contribute, when and if the company can meet the challenge of unlocking that capacity. Begin by looking at your business objectives over the next two years or so. What do you need from your people to achieve those objectives? You need people who are continuously learning and continuously applying that learning to the organization's most important work, the work that yields the competitive advantage. What's the smartest way to make that happen? Build a work environment where all employees are given real opportunities to maximize their potential, the guidance they need to feel confident enough to take risks, and the feedback they need to know how to improve their future performance. The guidelines and principles that support inclusion and a culture of development are not only the best business decision; they apply in any location.

    The huge turnover rates of call centers in India provide a case study for Quality Treatment in a different context. While Americans fret over the outsourcing of jobs to these call centers, their 40 per cent turnover rates suggests that the educated, bright and ambitious young workers realize the jobs offer no future. What does this fast-growing desire for better opportunities mean for those call centers and for the Indian economy? New opportunities for call center employees at their companies? Creation of new businesses of increasing sophistication? Greater emigration for better jobs in the West? An exploration of what constitutes Quality Treatment for these employees in India might decrease turnover and improve the long-term business performance of the call centers.

One executive summarized the competitive advantage that flows from an inclusive work environment and a culture of development:

You've got to make your company attractive to people in very different cultures and different time zones. How do I get the most I can out of every single person that works for us? How do we work effectively as a team? If we can do that, then the likelihood is that you're going to be pretty happy people, and you're going to love working here.

2. **Discuss the proposition that any circumstance hindering employees from maximizing their capabilities or causing employees to divert their focus from the company's business goals is a lost business opportunity.** Framing the issue this way allows even those inclined to resist to join in. Said one executive of a manufacturing company, after he'd had a lot of experience in the Middle East:

When we presented them [with] some really good thinking about things we'd done here and why we're doing them, we turned it [inclusion] into a good business practice. All of a sudden we're getting the workforce engaged. We got a huge halo effect.

We have sometimes found ourselves in the middle of vestiges of historical—and sometimes very current—battles between countries. These particular battles are not a part of our shared history in the West, but we have analogous experiences. Conversations from a place of exploration and openness rather than from a place of judgment can become the basis for establishing new norms of how we will work together. In Egypt, for example, we found Pakistanis who were chafing under subjective and unfair judgments of Indian supervisors. We cannot solve the border disputes between their two countries, but a respectful and insightful mediator can help them explore exactly what it is that pushes their buttons. What is the cost to the business of continuing this battle in the work environment? Then people on both sides can begin to recognize predictive behaviors and to use effective effort to shift the conversation onto the ground of shared business objectives.

Similarly, centuries-long enmities between China and Japan are losing some of their edge as Japanese companies acquire Chinese business interests, and vice versa. Familiarity, based on actual individual experiences and achieving shared business goals have refocused the discussions and lessened the impact of the tensions. It is a pattern familiar to most Americans, and the trend is equally clear in the Far East. Thriving and healthy cultures need the broadest range of new talent; openness will continue to expand. When we respect local cultural and historical experiences, understand more of how they came about, and have earned the trust of our new colleagues, we can facilitate inclusion and a culture of development with them.

We have not yet found many leaders, general managers or line managers who take issue with this reasoning behind Quality Treatment. Everyone wants a workforce that is as motivated and productive as possible. It is a short step from accepting the business paradigm about inclusion and a culture of development to realizing that anything limiting the investment in human capital diminishes the potential return.

3. **Begin a conversation about the salient barriers in the different culture—the Negative Treatment.** It takes time to understand your own biases, and it takes even more time to understand those of people in different cultures. The conversation begins by exploring your own biases and then moving on to a conversation about the salient barriers—the Negative Treatment—in a given culture. That conversation can be guided by open questions that encourage candid exchanges.

- What cultural beliefs, assumptions or practices might cloud our objective judgments at work?
- Could those judgments diminish a company's potential return?
- Where is the flow of ideas stopped?
- Are there certain people no one listens to?
- Are there certain people who have learned never to speak up?
- Are there people who are blocked at the door, without any hope of being hired?
- What is the loss to the business of creativity and market access from these decisions to exclude?

When you ask probing questions and listen with an open mind, honest dialogue can occur. A definition of Quality Treatment that is consistent with a particular culture can emerge. A note of caution: it is always dangerous to presume very much. We have found over and over again that you can never overestimate the importance of local culture in any business situation.

4. **Once there is realization, the slow process of changing be-
    havior can begin in a mutually respectful environment.**
    Using the concepts of Quality Treatment, Position and Dis-
    position, we proceed with subtlety and respect to uncover
    the sort-and-select processes at work in each new location—
    where the special few are identified quickly and targeted for
    development (the sort-and-select process is discussed in the
    Introduction and Chapter One)—and then figure out how
    to adjust those processes so they support rather than hin-
    der achievement of an organization's business objectives.
    The actual steps in any country will be unique to that set-
    ting, planned in a collaborative process with local leaders and
    those managers charged with implementing them on a daily
    basis.

    Here is an example of the potential business results
    from fostering an inclusive work environment. When a
    German bank acquired an American bank, one Ameri-
    can business unit head who was committed to inclusion
    put together his most creative and inclusion-experienced
    team. They already knew everything about their own work
    products. They then learned everything they could about
    what their German counterpart department did, as well as
    who was on that leadership team. In addition, they put to-
    gether a proposal for integrating the two business opera-
    tions which identified opportunities to create the greatest
    value—where services could be merged and where service
    offerings could be enhanced. When they met with the Ger-
    man team, they knew how to be flexible and open and how
    best to present their proposal. Their planning, which went
    beyond the typical financial analysis to encompass inclu-
    sion concepts, proved its worth within the first year. Their

department had not only the best performance in the merged entity but also a significant increase over the combined results of the two separate departments in the year prior to the merger. Paying attention to your people—inclusion—is a business strategy.

MANAGE INCLUSION

What have we discovered as we apply this four-step process to our discussions with leaders and managers around the world? We invariably find them excited by the business potential. The concepts of Negative Treatment, Quality Treatment, Position and Disposition are meaningful in any work environment.

To open the discussion we often use a video of an experiment conducted by public school teacher Jane Elliott over a period of a week in the 1960s in her classroom. In "A Class Divided," she divided her class into two groups, the first week making those with blue eyes the favored group and then switching the favorable treatment to those with brown eyes. In each case, the designated "lesser" group was identified by wearing literal blue collars, and their self-confidence and performance immediately declined almost in direct proportion to the increase in belittling and even cruel treatment by those students without a collar. This simple experiment among children reveals the power of express societal assumptions and the resulting Negative Treatment, and we can begin to identify the metaphoric collars in their own societies. Everyone connects with the experience, even today in all work environments.

What "collars" are undermining the ability of many employees in a different culture to maximize their contributions to a company's business? The collars we have found are varied:

functional (based on work departments) or related to language, bilingual ability, age, skin color, country of origin, education at certain schools or abroad, family background, caste, generation gaps, conditions of employment (such as part-time), disability, work styles, historical enmities, degrees of formality and informality, and—the issue that in one form or another crosses every border and culture—gender. We can understand these collars, even though we come from an American experience, and we find that after these discussions, others see our collars in a more generous light. The metaphor evokes cross-cultural understanding and forms the platform for more productive and honest interactions.

In Amsterdam at dinner with a client, for example, we were discussing her country's international reputation for tolerance when she revealed a Dutch "collar." She moved the salt and pepper shakers to opposite sides of the table and said, "We are tolerant as long as you are over there," and then, as she moved them back together, "but not so comfortable when you are here." When we start from a place of respect and exploration, honest acknowledgment can occur. Then it becomes possible to design a process that can achieve true inclusion and a real culture of development.

Because Quality Treatment rests on the belief that all employees are capable of making contributions toward achieving business results, the task of managers anywhere is to discover the conditions that inspire, encourage and allow employees to make those contributions. Managers in the West, for example, may use what we call "constructive feedback"—open, direct, generous and regular assessments of an employees work performance—to create that positive work environment (see Chapter 5 for a more thorough discussion of constructive feedback), but managers in Japan, where conformity makes civility possible in a crowded island country and where respect for elders and gracious and inexplicit verbal communication are central tenets of that civility, may need a different strategy. Trying to impose give-and-take within teams composed of superiors and their workers would probably not be productive. What culturally consistent behavior would encourage employees to improve their performance? Managers might find that asking for the opinions of younger employees and actively listening to them would produce similar results. Experience with workers from other countries, there to fill labor pool gaps caused by smaller-size Japanese families, is affording opportunities to explore new strategies for unlocking potential. So is the presence of non-Japanese English-language teachers in many Japanese secondary schools.

We have also found when we discuss the kind of environment where Quality Treatment thrives, we often open a door on novel ideas and solutions from surprising or unusual sources. One client learned that working in Nigeria.

I think many come to Africa from Europe and North America with a mindset of "deficit"—poor education, poor resources, poor training. The list goes on. The truth is the paradigm is wrong. I found incredibly resourceful people. When a piece of equipment breaks, we wait for the new parts to arrive, and when they don't, we blame customs, the company or anybody else. The Nigerians I worked with don't bother to wait or sit around and complain. They immediately begin working to copy, repair or modify what they have. In no time they're back to work. I saw this happen again and again, in all kinds of circumstances.

We know of many examples where close-minded managers lost business potential because they could not see the value of new ideas unless they came through appropriate channels. The Home Depot, the largest home repair and renovation store in the world, was started because the founders' prior boss dismissed their idea about a warehouse-type store where women would be welcome. The rest is history. A very healthy respect for what everyone brings to the table is not just talk. We all have a lot to contribute AND a lot to learn.

The concepts of Position and Disposition, so central to the practice of Quality Treatment, frequently reveal other productive new strategies. For example, many women in Japan work part-time in order to spend more time with their children, and these women are put on a sort of side-track at the office. This situation is not so different from the experience of many women in the U.S. We use the concepts of Position and Disposition as a framework for discussing this challenge, comparing the assignments and guidance a man might receive to the assignments and guidance accorded a woman. The group usually comes up with some strategies that push the envelope of their current management approaches, but also respect the prevalent cultural values and beliefs. These are liberating experiences for all employees, but especially for the younger participants.

Many large Chinese companies today, as huge and as cash rich as they are, are relatively recent inventions, rudimentary in organizational development and management techniques. They are the result of visionary and ambitious farmers who developed successful cooperatives in their own villages when new government policy began allowing individual income production. These farmers then left in droves to start businesses in the city. The scale of this migration is difficult to comprehend: China already has more than a hundred cities with populations that exceed one million, more than all other major cities in the world combined. There is every reason to believe these ambitious business entrepreneurs will quickly become adept at talking about and using Western management and organizational techniques in order to grow their businesses. It is also easy to predict that the Eastern style of communication—less direct, more subtle and more deferential—will influence the way business is conducted everywhere. China's consumption already drives many elements of the global economy, such as oil prices, and its potential impact is probably exponentially greater. Chinese culture is bound to influence the culture of business as well.

We believe over time and with continuing commitment, Negative Treatment can begin to recede and Quality Treatment to become more prevalent, just as it can and does where it has taken hold in the West. The challenge is to bring about good business results even where the styles of communication or of doing business are different. Starting from a place of judgment, a belief on each side that what I'm doing is right and what you are doing is wrong, compounds the difficulty. Starting from a place of openness and exploration, on the other hand, eventually forms the basis for establishing new norms about now we will work together. The process has never been, and will never be, quick or easy, because eliminating the power of deeply held but unproductive societal assumptions is a great challenge. No one knows that better than those of us in the U.S. who have wrestled with our own assumptions for four decades without yet reaching the goal of inclusion.

As societies begin to open up, the language about long-held judgments will change before the actual judgment is abandoned altogether. One strategy that can buffet early discomfort about the waves of change is to dice the old judgments into smaller and smaller pieces using new language. For example, potential workers from cities all around Shanghai are considered by some to be inferior. But now Shanghai's population is bursting at the seams, and these cities are growing by leaps and bounds. With technological advantages and award-winning architecture, many of them are becoming desirable, even trendy, places to live, especially for ambitious and adventurous younger people. The definition of inferiority had to be refined: were you born in those cities, or did you choose to move there when you were already working? Before too many decades, no one will even be aware of any assumption about inferiority.

We know from our own experience as well as feedback from clients that our process works. One HR executive who's had a lot of global experience talks about his company's success with inclusion, Negative and Quality Treatment, Position and Disposition:

> It's more than just another diversity program. It is about getting the most out of all our people. We suspected it had legs well beyond the U.S., and it does. It's very popular.

ENLIST LOCAL LEADERSHIP TO SPEAK OUT AND MODEL BEHAVIOR

In any company anywhere in the world, inclusion will only be achieved with the support of the leadership. Having local leaders speak publicly, write articles in company newsletters and attend any training sessions, stressing personal experiences about exclusion and commitment to inclusion, will begin to create an effective learning environment. Since people can always sense when the leadership commitment is authentic, words are only the first steps. Modeling inclusive behavior should become a normal part of day-to-day activities. The critical aspect of "selling" inclusion globally, therefore, actually mirrors the U.S. experience.

How do you get the local leadership on board? By making the business case to them in a manner that respects where they are. One global bank bought a small but very profitable bank in Korea in order to gain a foothold in that important but exclusive market culture. The acquiring bank leadership team learned about Korean culture, the many fault lines of education, class and family background, and planned its face-to-face meeting with the Korean bank leadership carefully. They chose to keep the Korean leaders in place; after all, they were already successful. There was no sense of Westerners coming in to take over; rather, they positioned the new relationship as a new opportunity to build an international brand. They even made sure that one of their visiting team spoke Korean, and they provided translation headsets for everyone, which greatly facilitated the personal interactions. In this atmosphere they were able to convince the leaders of the business case for inclusion and the importance of their active participation in achieving it. This foresight not only smoothed the integration of the two companies' businesses; it may have opened the door to a new and inclusive work environment. Commitment and time will tell the answer to that challenge.

DESIGN HUMAN RESOURCES PROCEDURES TO FACILITATE INCLUSION

We have found that when human resources departments are fully engaged as companies plan and think about the challenges of doing business in a new culture, the outcomes improve, both

initially and over time. If inclusion is a part of the up-front
strategic planning, and integrated solutions are designed, the
inevitable and predictable problems down the road are avoided,
along with the far greater time and resources needed to recover
from them. The experiences in global business mirror the experiences within our home base, the U.S. We have found the
following steps to be most helpful.

1. **Make sure employees have what they need to establish
   themselves in a safe and supportive environment.** Of course
   this includes shelter, but shelter is not enough. We know of
   a woman geologist whose company wanted her to accept a
   position in one of their Middle Eastern operations. While her
   company arranged for her housing, she was left on her own
   to make many other major arrangements. One of those ne-
   cessities was applying for a residency permit for her husband
   as soon as she arrived. She was shocked to learn it was denied;
   this country would not accept a woman as the primary wage
   earner. Because this was an important career-building assignment for her, she and her husband lived apart for five years.
   Now her company knows how to circumvent this prohibi-
   tion. HR has the ability to research these factors in advance
   and, we believe, a duty to protect employees from this kind of
   hardship.

2. **Show respect for local language.** This means more than actual translation, which is important; it includes understanding appropriate verbal discourse in the new culture.

   Misunderstandings based on inept translations mean the
   discussion starts on a note of confusion and sometimes even
   resistance. For example, who can forget the embarrassment

of GM when it marketed its Chevy Nova in South America, completely unaware that "no va" in Spanish meant "it doesn't go? The literal translation into Spanish of "inclusion" is so newly related to the business world that no one understood what it meant. Some South American corporate officers, who understood both the corporate message and local usage, stepped in and began to refer to it as "participación." Even where English is the first language, spelling must be checked, since the same words can be spelled differently. In the Middle East and in Asia, where even the alphabet is different, precise language becomes more critical and challenging, and it does not matter that most of the people Westerners do business with can communicate in English. These simple displays of respect for the local language are so easy to accomplish that, once recognized, it is hard to understand why every HR department doesn't attend to them. Respect for language fosters good business relationships.

The English-language training received by Indian employees hired to work in call centers is a good example of an effective HR program. Every company supplements the extensive English lessons most employees have had in school with lessons on regional American accents. And they go further. Employees learn idiosyncrasies of Western customers, for example, information about sports in Britain and the U.S., and American dining habits. Anyone who has connected with one of these call center employees knows how much these lessons improve customer service.

Beyond actual translations, HR needs to be sensitive to the use of language in the new culture. Is formality an important sign of respect here? This issue trips up many Americans especially, who pride themselves on their informality. One company we work with trained employees dealing with Nigerian businesses in how to write culturally appropriate emails.

The first level, employees learned, is attention to clarity and avoiding acronyms and idioms. The next level, however, is even more important. In Nigeria, showing respect for status, education and experience are paramount, so a formal and dignified presentation is expected. You would never address a business associate there by the first name, but only as Dr., Mr. or Mrs. In addition, you had better introduce yourself in the same context, letting the recipient know your educational background and experience, for instance. Building the relationship matters.

These same issues surface as more and more meetings are virtual rather than face-to-face, especially in global companies such as energy and oil companies who conduct business across fifteen time zones. Thoughtful companies know they have to find the budget for at least one face-to-face meeting in order to establish the relationships. After that, virtual meetings are possible, even productive, but in each session all must pay attention to the relationship before turning to task.

3. **Provide a safe haven for exploring cultural differences.** Glib words about inclusion or respecting and valuing difference are not any more effective around the world than they are in the West. Failure to account for the actual differences and incorporate them into any relationship-building initiatives will not make them disappear. Understanding and trust can only come from moving through these sometimes painful conversations. Throughout Africa, for instance,

where ethnicity remains vibrant and significant, Westerners can be uncomfortable talking about it, just as they are uncomfortable talking about race at home. The ethnic differences, however, cannot be glossed over. One HR executive we know therefore addressed the issue head-on when she arrived in Cameroon.

I asked one of my new employees to think of herself as a representative of her country. How would she describe that? She was silent, and I thought perhaps I had made a terrible mistake. But she finally said she didn't know how to answer my question. "I can't think of it as one culture—there are too many ethnicities."

The fact that she did not get an answer was not important; the gap was bridged; the conversation had begun.

Another HR manager used a similar technique when he arrived in Nigeria. He knew ahead of time that names had great significance, indicating status, family history, education and achievement. He did not make the mistake of shortening or familiarizing names, as we do so quickly in the West. Instead, he asked a group of new employees to describe what their names meant. He thus began a lively conversation, where much information was exchanged in an atmosphere of awareness and respect.

4. **Pay attention to how women are treated.** Gender discrimination is evident to Westerners throughout most of the world, but many societies do not yet see it as an issue. It is manifested in surprising and unexpected ways, as well as more obvious ones, and the utmost care is required in even talking about it.

One executive from Taiwan we worked with told us proudly that he had three companies, and one would go to each of his sons. His daughter, however, would have to marry well or go to a professional school, such as law or medicine, because she could not possibly be a business executive. He did not see any problem with his plan.

The policy of only one child per couple in China is perhaps a more extreme example. It has led to a gender imbalance; there are far fewer women than men in the younger generations. Unlike most other places in the world, the Chinese labor pool in at least one regard is becoming less diverse. This is a workplace issue of almost unimaginable magnitude for China's future.

When one realizes that women have only been able to vote and own property in the West for less than a century, the viewpoint of the rest of the world is not surprising or even all that far removed from Western experience. One Chief Diversity Officer at a global financial firm described many heated discussions with her British counterpart, who insisted the U.K. was free of gender issues. She still remembers clearly when he called her one night at home to say the issue had finally "hit his radar screen." His chairman had become concerned about the huge turnover among women and the lack of women at the top. He was convinced these facts would hinder the firm's ability to serve and maintain their clients, and he had to reverse the trends. "Gender," she declared, "is an issue that's pretty much the same across all countries and all cultures."

In Spain, in the Far East, Southeast Asia, South America and the Middle East, we usually receive firm denials when we first ask about women—"We don't have that problem here."

Invariably the group of participants protesting is all-male, except for possibly one or two women who remain silent. Our job is to find a way to deliver Quality Treatment to women in the workplace in a manner that is acceptable in that culture.

Another executive we work with describes one approach he has found effective in opening the discussion about gender:

I made a presentation to our HR leaders from Asia, Europe, Latin America, the Middle East, about what we do in the U.S. around work/life balance. Does any of this stuff sound familiar? Is any of this stuff of value? Does any of this resonate? Of course! We've got tons of challenges with women in the workforce. We could really use some more balance.

5. **Design trainings and their interactive exercises to show respect for and understanding of local cultural mores.** We knew our training curriculum had to be translated as well as adapted to each local culture, but we learned the hard way that interactive exercises have to be even more carefully crafted to fit what is acceptable. Sometimes the issue is obvious, for example, in predominantly Muslim cultures, card games are frowned upon. But other issues are buried deeper. In some parts of Asia, we found role-playing counterproductive. "Saving face" makes it too embarrassing to perform out of character in front of a group. The most difficult change for us was designing games where no one comes out a clear winner. We have fun with competition, but other cultures are more attuned to outward humility. In India, for

example, displaying individual aggressiveness is considered
gauche and impolite. When you are aware of these cultural
differences, you can adapt both content and exercises to incorporate local concepts and issues, as well as relevant examples, activities and experiences.

We are convinced that the assumptions and behaviors
underlying inclusion and a culture of development are as
relevant around the world as they are in the West. Negative
Treatment, Quality Treatment, Position and Disposition are
effective guides to improved productivity everywhere, so
long as they are introduced in culturally appropriate contexts, and after establishing a mutually respectful relationship. The needle measuring change moves gradually, just as
it does in the West. But there is low-hanging fruit for those
who study in advance, listen with a keen ear and observe
with a respectful eye.

CHAPTER EIGHT

Measuring Progress And Demonstrating Results

...I need to convince my CEO or he won't support it.

HR Director

Everything we've discussed up to this point has emphasized the business benefits of building and sustaining an inclusive culture of development. But our experience tells us that many readers will have a healthy skepticism about our assertions. They will want proof. Others who accept the benefits may still need proof because they have to demonstrate concrete results to their leaders. They are in a position similar to a newly appointed HR director who said to us at a recent conference:

Our CEO told me he wants some proof that inclusion produces business results. How do I do this? I know in my bones inclusion makes an important difference, but I need to convince my CEO or he won't support it.

A key aspect of all effective business strategies is determining whether or not they have achieved their goals, and building inclusion and a culture of development is no different. This chapter provides assessment and evaluation guidelines that will enable you to measure progress and demonstrate results. We focus on measuring changes in individual behavior at work that lead to improved performance, such as increased overall assessment ratings, as well as evidence of improved productivity in the company overall in the following categories.

- Increased breadth of recruitment;
- Increased internal sourcing and advancement;
- Increased diversity across the board;
- Reduced turnover;
- Improved employee satisfaction;
- Improved customer satisfaction; and
- Increased market share.

THE PLACE TO BEGIN

The first step is to benchmark where you are. This means collecting and analyzing relevant data on your organization's current situation. Why bother? There are three reasons:

- to provide a baseline against which you can document change;
- to highlight existing strengths, so your change initiative can build upon them; and

- to reveal areas that suggest improvement is needed, so you can fashion the most effective strategies for addressing them.

In Chapter Four, *Strategic Leadership*, we discussed some of the information that leaders can use to better understand their organization's current state with regard to inclusion and development. In Chapter One, *Two Models of Development*, and Chapter Five, *Aligning Human Resources with a Culture of Development*, we discussed the information HR leaders can collect to benchmark inclusion and development. Here we add to that body of information in order to compile a complete background picture. The most useful data falls into four categories:

- business;
- organizational;
- development and advancement; and
- employee feedback.

Even if your organization does not have current data in each of these areas, we recommend you begin with whatever data is available and then design a process for collecting the rest. We also recommend collecting the data for the organization overall and slicing it according to age, gender, race, ethnicity, disability and other diversity categories because, as we have discussed in every chapter, the experience of these diverse categories is the bellwether for experience of almost everyone. Finally, we recommend you slice the data again, according to job title, level, department, function and any other organizational variable you deem relevant.

Business Data

- Sales and Marketing data on market share within emerging markets, including those defined by gender, age, race, ethnicity, sexual orientation and other key demographic variables. This data can be compared with available data from competitor organizations. Such data may be in the form .of survey analyses collected from various industry sectors by independent or membership organizations as well as projections of future trends and opportunities, for example from multiple government sources.
- External customer satisfaction and retention data along with the costs—real and potential—of losing customers.
- Productivity and profitability overall, as well as by specific functional group, division and/or business unit.

Organizational Data

- A demographic profile of the organization in terms of levels and functional areas, with concrete data on the distribution of members of disenfranchised groups by job level, function and department, as well as the age distribution. Data which cannot be determined without asking direct questions to employees requires preparation. Some employees may become suspicious or uncomfortable being asked certain questions, so it is important to begin by laying the leadership's communications groundwork for the overall initiative as described in Chapter 4 (*Strategic Leadership*). In addition, we recognize the potential legal risk involved in collecting some of this data, particularly in the U.S. But you cannot plan a journey, let alone measure or make progress on it, if you don't know your starting point.

And the ability to document progress on the road to an inclusive culture of development may be the best defense to any discrimination lawsuit.

- Recruitment data, including entry-level and lateral hires, with special emphasis on every variation of diversity within the candidate pools and among those selected.
- Retention and turnover data—both voluntary and involuntary, paying special attention to any disproportionate turnover rates by functional area, level or diversity group. In addition, data should be gathered to quantify the costs of replacing an employee at different levels and functions in the organization.
- The number of inclusion and development-related grievances lodged and legal actions filed, analyzed by job level, department and function, age, race, ethnicity, gender and other diverse groups as well as any other relevant variables. In addition, the potential and actual costs of resolving grievances and legal actions should be calculated using traditional risk assessment formulas.

Development and Advancement Data

- The distribution of key development opportunities by age, gender, race, ethnicity and other relevant diversity variables. The opportunities to be analyzed include cross-group rotational placements, company core business-related key assignments, accelerated development programs and external development programs, such as the leadership programs offered by many universities.
- Advancement and succession planning data, including the actual selection process, along with the criteria used in selection,

and whether or not there is a diverse feeder pool of candidates for the key positions.

Employee Feedback Data: Quantitative and Qualitative

- Employee satisfaction surveys zero in on relevant inclusion issues such as leadership commitment, recruitment, work environment, supervision, learning and development, advancement, as well as personal perception. We quantify reactions to statements such as:

  Leaders demonstrate their commitment to diversity and inclusion by their actions as well as their words.

  I believe my diverse background will not hinder my advancement in this organization.

  It is rare in my work environment to hear negative comments or jokes based on ethnicity, gender, race and/or sexual orientation.

While these surveys cannot explore issues in depth, they do identify issues and have the added advantage of providing every employee a platform for voicing his or her opinion. We recommend survey results include comparisons by all key demographic and organizational variables, such as level and functional group or department, as well as by age, gender, race, ethnicity and other diversity groups.

- Upward appraisal surveys, where employees evaluate their managers, and 360-degree feedback surveys, where all people who interact with a particular employee—above, below, beside—are asked to evaluate his or her performance—provide feedback on behavior relevant to building and sustaining an inclusive culture of development. Examples of statements about a particular employee to which we gauge reactions in these survey processes are:

   Treats all employees fairly, regardless of their diverse background.

   Works well with people who have perspectives, backgrounds, styles and/or opinions different from his or her own.

   Seeks out the diverse perspectives, ideas and work products of others to accomplish objectives.

   Encourages others to stay open to, seek and learn from diverse perspectives.

   Treats all people in the work environment with respect.

   Openly addresses work-related diversity issues with employees.

- Qualitative interviews and focus groups with employees at all levels explore more fully perceptions and experiences relevant to inclusion and development. They allow more in-depth discussions on issues that have been identified statistically through employee satisfaction surveys.

For example, if survey data indicate that most employees of color state they believe their race is an obstacle to development, focus groups with representative employees of color can uncover the specific experiences that have shaped that perception. In focus groups we use more open-ended questions to encourage discussion:

Why do you think so many employees of color responded to the survey statement this way?

What are some examples of employees of color given fewer opportunities?

What have your own experiences been?

What specific changes would be necessary to convince you that employees of color have fair opportunities to develop in this organization?

The combination of quantitative and qualitative data underlies the most reliable initial benchmarks and measurements of progress over time. Therefore we believe our multi-level approach to collecting actionable employee feedback is the best foundation from which to build effective organizational responses and forward-reaching initiatives.

The value of quantitative survey data is twofold. First, it allows maximum participation by employees because the entire organization is polled. The responses can be easily sorted according to any organizational and diversity variables deemed relevant. Second, it provides quantitative data that numbers-oriented organizational leaders and managers may more readily accept as valid. We fully realize that many business-minded people see numbers as being more objective than words.

There are, however, limitations to quantitative survey data. While positive ratings reveal the organization's current strengths, and negative ratings reveal the areas that need improvement, the results rarely shed light on the "whys" or the root causes, let alone the best way to solve them. Take, for example, one of the most consistent negative responses we receive: "In this company, 'who you know' is usually more important for advancement than 'what you know.'"

Even if 80 per cent of the respondents agree with this statement, we don't know what, specifically, is driving their common conclusion; many different experiences could lead to the same response. We recommend follow-up data be collected through in-depth interviews and/or focus groups, because those strategies shed light on the experiences behind the perceptions, both positive and negative. In some cases, the negative responses followed continued disappointment on applications for different positions, when the successful candidate seemed less qualified:

I've been in the "feeder pool" for promotion for five years. Less qualified people have come and gone. I guess I'm just not hooked up with the right VPs.

In other cases focus group participants expressed frustration with the job posting system because they saw how easily it could be circumvented.

*I know for a fact that managers have HR describe the job
so the person they want is about the only one who fits the
description.*

In companies where constructive feedback has begun to
become a part of the culture, we hear about different results.

*I felt I was given opportunities to develop, along with
very useful coaching and feedback after I was denied a
promotion. I took the advice, and the next time around I
got the position I applied for.*

Quantitative survey data suggest areas that warrant further investigation or strengths that can be built upon; qualitative data provides in-depth understanding about why people
respond as they do. The first two quoted comments suggest
a relatively simple solution to internal sourcing through job
postings: enforcing the spirit of the program already in place
by holding managers accountable for their decisions and
holding HR accountable for the process. The third suggests
the benefits that lie ahead. Broad communication of real data
about better results will also neutralize negative perceptions
based on ad hoc observations or gut feelings. Not all perceptions are easily neutralized or addressed but, in general, if employees feel their concerns are heard and there are good-faith
efforts to address them, they will commit to more effective
effort at work, and progress in productivity will be achieved.

The data sources described in this section help an organization benchmark exactly where it is, both positive and negative,
so initiatives in response are based on realistic and appropriate

goals that support both an inclusive culture of development and improved organizational productivity.

MEASURING BEHAVIOR CHANGE

We now turn to what we believe should be a major component of strategies to measure progress toward the overall goal: behavior change. Our starting point is the widely used and highly regarded human resources program evaluation model put forth by psychologist Donald Kirkpatrick in 1959, and his model has become the industry standard in the human resources and training communities. Kirkpatrick posited people evidence learning at four progressive levels. Over the decades, his model has been applied to a much broader range of learning strategies. Business, for example, has shifted the ultimate focus from the response of the learner to the response of the business: measuring return on investment (ROI). What are the business goals the intervention addressed, the critical output indicators, to adapt Six Sigma language? What was the business outcome? The model we use, therefore, has five levels, to reflect corporate leaders' very real concern with ROI, including investment in human capital:

- Participant Reaction—initial response to the learning intervention at its conclusion (often referred to as "happy sheets");
- Knowledge Gained—statement of what new information you acquired as a result of the intervention, independent of using that information;
- Behavior Change—how over time participants have used what they learned in the intervention to improve their work performance;

- Business Impact—evidence of overall improvement in work performance and other HR markers such as turnover and employee satisfaction; and
- Return on Investment—linking improved performance to more traditional business profitability markers such as customer satisfaction and market share.

Figure 8.1, Evaluating the Effectiveness of Interventions, depicts how each of these levels adds depth to the experience gained at the prior level:

Level 5 Return on Investment

Level 4 Business Impact

Level 3 Behavior Change

Level 2 Knowledge Gained

Level 1 Participant Reaction

Figure 8.1: Evaluating the Effectiveness of Interventions

We focus our discussion here on Levels 3-5, measuring changes in individual behavior and then applying those results to overall organizational goals. What do employees experience when they're on their daily jobs and no longer in the safer environment of on-site or off-site training, or in the excitement of rolling out a new initiative?

Take, for example, a diversity and inclusion workshop for all of a company's managers and supervisors. Participants may have a great experience in the workshop (Level 1) and leave with a much better understanding of inclusion (Level 2), but a culture of development will not become "the way we do business" unless or until these managers apply the new concepts and practice the new skills in a work environment where they are encouraged to do so in their daily behavior. Only then does the desired culture change occur. It is difficult for us to understand why anyone would essentially throw away the cost of such a training by failing to incorporate the concepts and practices into its overall organizational culture.

The key measurement tools for documenting behavior change are 180-degree, 360-degree, and other feedback instruments. They are particularly useful when administered both before and after specific interventions or events, so that comparisons with the "control group" can demonstrate behavior change and identify strengths as well as areas that still need improvement. We are aware that some experts have a negative view of 360-degree feedback tools, but our examination has invariably found poor planning and poor implementation to be the cause of dissatisfaction rather than some problem with the technique itself.

Some companies and their leaders will view reaching Level 3 as sufficient to demonstrate the positive results of their inclusion/development initiatives. Their professional opinion, often supported by personal experience and empirical observation, is that if behavior has become more inclusive across the board, more employees will be developed and better able to contribute to the bottom-line. Since behavior change is key to creating an inclusive environment, this is a significant and valid approach to evaluating the success of specific interventions such as skill-based training or mentoring.

Other companies may want to go even further, to document the impact of their interventions on specific organizational indicators (Level 4) and/or return on investment (Level 5). In those efforts, we find it remains necessary to document Level 3 outcomes first, because Level 3 success is the foundation for measuring outcomes at both Level 4 and Level 5. Figure 8.2, From Inclusion to ROI, illustrates the cumulative relationship among inclusion and development interventions, behavior change and business impact/ROI.

| Diversity/Inclusion Initiative | → | Behavior Change | → | Business Impact |

Figure 8.2: From Inclusion to ROI

Some business leaders may argue that any link between learning interventions and behavior changes associated with inclusion and a culture of development on the one hand and business results and ROI on the other is unconvincing. It is true that bottom-line results—like productivity, profitability and market share—are affected by many variables, both internal and external to the organization, so it is difficult to determine the impact of any one specific factor on such macro-level outcomes. This challenge, therefore, is not unique to inclusion.

Even when such inclusion and development interventions coincide with an improvement in business performance, we can only declare an association or correlation, not a cause-and-effect relationship. Naysayers and skeptics can and will remain unconvinced that inclusion and development played a role in bringing about the improvement but, again, this challenge is not unique to inclusion and development. Both marketing and accounting, for example, began facing the same cause-and-effect challenges, but they are now universally accepted, even though it is nearly impossible to isolate the impact of either on bottom-line results.

We have found most companies acknowledge there is some benefit rather than spend the extraordinary amount of time and resources necessary to draw the cause-and-effect relationship for something they consider obvious. Leaders who are already committed to inclusion and development of all employees fall into this category; they see no need to demonstrate what, to them, is a clear and obvious benefit. We are not surprised by this response, because diversity in nature as well as in investment is a universally accepted value, and we posit that diversity among human beings is equally valuable. Creating a laboratory-type setting where most of the variables affecting the outcome can be controlled is simply not a sensible use of limited resources. Sears did make such an attempt and decided the cost far outweighed any possible additional proof to be gained from the analysis. Other companies forgo the analysis because they don't have the data systems in place and don't want to expend the resources—time and money—to establish them.

CASE STUDY: TWO COMPANIES

Whether or not an individual company decides to isolate the specific cause-and-effect relationship, we urge all companies to embed measurement into each phase of their inclusion and development initiatives. You need to know your starting point so you know whether or not you're headed in the right direction. Without the rigor of measurements, you will never be able to demonstrate any impact on more traditional business indicators. Take the example of two companies, both committed to building inclusion and a culture of development. Employee surveys and focus groups at both companies found almost two-thirds of all employees agreed or strongly agreed that "who you know" is often more important for advancement than "what you know," and the percentage rose to almost three-fourths among women and more than 80 per cent among employees of color.

Based on these results, both companies decided to put all managers and supervisors through a two-day inclusion workshop, but they wanted to see concrete business results from the training investment. They both began by collecting baseline data on two key business indicators: turnover and productivity, and they both planned to assess improvements beginning one year after the training.

The only difference between the processes put in place by the two companies was the second company's use of a 360-degree feedback tool as part of its inclusion workshop. That company's participants, therefore, were able to evaluate themselves and receive feedback from others on their inclusion-related behaviors as the new initiative began. These reports established a baseline—a clear picture of where these employees were as individuals, and in the aggregate probably provided a better understanding of why they behaved as they did as well as insight into how the company practices and procedures actually supported those behaviors.

Immediately following the training, participants in both companies rated the experience very positively. What happened one year out? The first company, where there was no baseline, failed to find much change in turnover and productivity overall. In addition, they could not determine whether or not the individuals who had been trained had changed their behavior, and they were not closer to identifying organizational barriers to improved performance. Informally, managers and supervisors shared their frustration with what they perceived to be barriers, but because these barriers had never been formally identified or acknowledged, no one could even suggest a plan to change them. We do not conclude from this scenario that the training failed, but it is clear that training by itself is not a magic bullet. We see it as one strategy that, when used in concert with other strategies, can be an effective part of achieving the goal.

The second company achieved far more satisfactory results, when it followed up the initial 360s with a second set a year after the training had been completed.

- At the outset of the workshop, managers had concrete feedback that they could apply to the concepts and skills presented in the sessions. This feedback was enormously helpful in developing action plans to be carried out after the workshop.
- The feedback data provided the means for establishing accountability—documenting whether managers were actually following through with their action plans and behaving more inclusively, according to their own account as well as the accounts of their supervisors, peers and direct reports. It is also important to note that in this company feedback data was positioned as valuable information for development and continuous improvement rather than as punishment for managers who failed to measure up.
- When sorted by division, the follow-up feedback data revealed that managers and supervisors in some parts of the company were having a more difficult time implementing what they had learned in the workshop. Their willingness and commitment had been met with obstacles that were beyond their control—for example, the forced ranking performance

management system described in Chapter 5. A series of focus groups with a representative sample of these managers and supervisors then presented the opportunity to discuss the identified organizational barriers and then to fashion steps to remove them.

Learning interventions such as training are helpful in building and sustaining a diverse and inclusive work environment, but no one intervention is sufficient. They are only effective as part of an overall effort, where, for example, HR policies and procedures that can either support or impede the implementation of inclusive behaviors are identified and addressed. By encouraging behavior change and simultaneously eliminating organizational barriers to behavior change, for example, companies can create an environment where inclusive behavior will flourish. These barriers include, but are not limited to, recruitment and selection, performance appraisal, reward and recognition systems, and promotion and advancement processes, all discussed in Chapter One, *Two Models of Development*, and Chapter 5, *Aligning Human Resources with a Culture of Development*.

- Because of the 360-degree feedback reports, individually and in the aggregate, the company was able to document a positive correlation between the behavior change of managers and supervisors at the division level and the key business indicators of productivity and turnover.

We find measuring behavior change to be a key factor in the success of any intervention designed to promote a culture of development, whether the intervention was expanding recruitment efforts, creating an inclusion council, implementing a mentoring

program or establishing a succession planning process. Therefore, for every intervention, we recommend the following:

- Decide which behavioral competencies your employees need for you to achieve your goals.
- Provide the education needed to master those behaviors, whether on-the-job training, skill building,
  mentoring or coaching needed to master those behaviors, and then hold people accountable for living
  them in their daily work.
- Track behavior change through 180-degree or 360-
  degree feedback tools. If your goal is to achieve inclusive behavior change (Level 3), these tools provide
  all the information you need to declare success.
- If your goal is to document business results (Level
  4) and/or ROI (Level 5), continue the analysis to
  show the correlation between documented behavior
  change and positive changes in organizational indicators. When managed well, the changes in inclusion and development behavior should accompany
  bottom-line performance indicators such as productivity, increased sales, increased market share and
  increased customer satisfaction.

INTEGRATING MEASUREMENT INTO YOUR INITIATIVE

Companies need to coordinate many steps to ensure the success
of any inclusion or development initiative. The Measurement

Grid, Figure 8.3, summarizes the process we recommend for integrating measurement into your initiatives.

Figure 8.3: Measurement Grid

	What	Why	How
Planning	**Step 1**—Set relevant, realistic, measurable goals.	To clarify "Why we are doing this" and what success will look like.	Assess the current situation using existing data via surveys, focus groups, interviews.
	Decide what behavior change supports the goals and how to measure this.	Inclusive behavior is necessary for the success of most interventions.	Select appropriate tools to document behavior.
	Determine if Levels 4 and/or 5 will be included in documenting results.	To reach consensus on success criteria and how to document them.	Calculate feasibility and costs/benefits of evaluating at Levels 4 and/or 5.
	Step 2—Establish accountability and reward success.	To ensure that interventions will be implemented as they were designed.	Link accountability to documented behavior change. Develop reward system consistent with organizational practices.

Implementation	**Step 3**—Monitor the implementation process.	To ensure that interventions will be implemented as they were designed.	Establish process "check points" and data sources. Monitor, make any necessary process adjustments.
Evaluation of Outcomes	**Step 4**—Document results.	To demonstrate that the intervention met its goals and success criteria.	Apply evaluation process developed in planning phase. Follow through with recognition/ reward and continuous improvement.

What follows is a more detailed discussion of each step of the process.

Step 1. Planning: Set Relevant, Realistic and Measurable Goals

Common sense tells us that if we don't know where we're going, we won't know if or when we have arrived. Yet many companies launch inclusion and development initiatives with action, never taking the time to understand their real issues and opportunities. As a result, time, money and other resources may be wasted going in wrong directions, on ineffective or irrelevant interventions. The error, of course, wastes more than those quantifiable resources because it can reinforce any skepticism that exists among some people in the organization about the ultimate value of inclusion and a culture of development.

We, therefore, strongly urge every company to begin by assessing the current situation and then move on to defining objectives, identifying improvement opportunities, developing realistic, measurable goals and designing targeted interventions.

Just as we outlined in Chapter 4, *Strategic Leadership*, Chapter 5, *Aligning Human Resources with a Culture of Development*, and earlier in this chapter, we recommend companies begin their assessment by examining existing business and human resource data and then identifying and collecting any relevant or useful additional data. In some instances, the issues and opportunities will be clear-cut:

- the company is experiencing excessive turnover among highly talented women;
- important customers are demanding to be served by more diverse professional teams;
- there are dysfunctional culture clashes between U.S. and non-U.S. employees in a global company; or
- the company perceives an opportunity to gain market share or to capture a new market niche.

But even with such clear-cut opportunities for improvement, effective and efficient strategies and interventions cannot be designed until the root causes are plumbed.

- Why are our best women leaving? To assume there are no organizational issues and they simply chose to stay home with children, for example, is not an adequate investigation.

- Why do we not present diverse professional teams? Why did we fail to perceive this as an issue?
- Why did we fail to perceive culture clashes as an issue? Why did we fail to plan adequately?
- Why did we fail to identify the market niche?

Each of these questions suggests the need to understand some basic attitudes and assumptions that underlie individual as well as organizational behavior. In order to design effective solutions to these gaps in perception, that represent unnecessary expense or even lost revenue, companies may need to gather additional data, either quantitative (for example, surveys) or more in-depth qualitative data (for example, one-on-one interviews and focus groups).

We have seen many companies waste resources or lose revenues because they were relying on incorrect assumptions. For example, one company's leaders recognized that their people of color were experiencing a higher turnover rate. They did not investigate the reasons because they assumed they left because competitors offered more lucrative financial packages. They, therefore, believed there was little they could do to alter the outcome. However, when they finally did begin to investigate, using focus groups with current employees and follow-up telephone interviews with recently departed employees, they were surprised. The real causes were the company's failure to make them feel included or to promote their development. For example, over and over, the interviewed people of color expressed concern that there was no mentoring for them and few of them were ever promoted. One former employee clearly described the problem of a work environment that was not perceived as welcoming.

I need someone high up whose office I can go into and close the door. That won't happen here.

The financial package was not the issue; offering them more money would have been counterproductive. The irony is that the real solution was relatively cost free.

In other cases, a company may want to initiate an inclusion and development effort proactively but may not know where to begin. Here, too, assessment tools such as employee surveys, interviews and/or focus groups, along with relevant organizational data, focus the discussion, identifying existing strengths as well as improvement opportunities.

Once the specific strengths and opportunities are identified and the goals defined, a company can design interventions that directly align with those goals and can put in place measurements that correspond to the desired results. Once again, the company can decide to focus on documented behavior changes that promote an inclusive environment (Level 3), or it can go further to document business impact (Level 4), and return on investment (Level 5).

Demonstrating the direct business benefits and return on investment of inclusion and development interventions depends on a number of interrelated factors, including:

- The type of industry and transparency of factors that influence the bottom line;
- The current state of a company's data systems—both operational and human resources;
- The willingness on the part of the company's leaders to invest time and other resources to undertake a measurement project.

A strategic HR, along with inclusion and development specialists, can educate corporate decision-makers about challenges as well as how to design the most effective and efficient interventions and measurement strategies.

Step 2. Planning: Establish Accountability and Reward Success

Everybody knows "What gets measured gets done" and the other side of that coin, "If it's not important enough to get measured, then it's not important enough to do." In today's results-driven workplaces, most employees have a full plate and then some. Requiring them to participate in new activities and, in many cases, to change their behavior, may be met with some resistance, even among those who agree philosophically with the changes and the ultimate goal. If companies cannot overcome this initial resistance, attempts to build inclusion and a culture of development will never be able to deliver the expected results.

How do companies ensure the desired behavioral changes? In the long run, the changes will be the result of a culture of development, where all employees live those values. But in the first instance, the answer is holding everyone accountable. We know of one company which spent over a million dollars putting all of its managers through an inclusion workshop. Although the workshop was well received and evaluated very positively—"the most valuable training this company has ever offered"—and inclusion competencies were integrated into the company's 360-degree reviews as a part of the annual performance management process, little changed in the company over the next few years.

When a new senior executive who championed inclusion and development joined the company, he found the answer.

Organizational data demonstrated that there was no correlation between a manager's inclusion scores and formal recognition or reward. He concluded that managers were asked to change their behaviors, sometimes in significant ways, but they were actually being rewarded for very different activities—primarily meeting traditional business goals.

The new executive then personally sponsored system changes that held managers accountable: 360-degree inclusion scores were factored into performance evaluations and decisions about both advancement and compensation. Needless to say, managers quickly discovered a revitalized commitment to inclusion and development results.

When a serious commitment is in evidence, everyone understands the recommended behaviors and the importance of demonstrating them.

Step 3. Implementation: Monitor the Process

Once the overall goals have been defined and communicated and integration of the relevant behavioral changes into the work environment has begun, monitoring the process kicks into gear, especially if companies want to be able to document business impact and ROI. The first steps are often referred to as "process measures," those monitored over time, such as the number of employees, sliced by membership into diverse groups as well as department and function, who attend development training, or the number of times an assigned mentor meets with his or her protégé. Participant evaluations of an initiative (Level 1) can also be viewed as a process measure.

Process measures have been criticized as meaningless, when, for example, they are mistakenly offered as proof of the success of the intervention. Such measurements do not prove the success of the intervention, but at the same time we caution against throwing the baby out with the bathwater. Process measures become meaningful when they are seen as opportunities for course correction. In any business initiative, experience along the way reveals appropriate or necessary modifications, and inclusion and development are no different. In fact, such modifications are almost the definition of cultures of development, where modifications that lead to continuous improvement are the ultimate goals.

To illustrate the value of process measures and course correction in the context of inclusion and development, we recall our experience with a newly implemented mentoring program at one company. A process measure—a focus group with protégés—uncovered a lot of dissatisfaction in interactions with assigned mentors. Protégés reported they were having difficulty scheduling regular meetings, and when they did meet, the mentors did most of the talking, so protégé issues were seldom discussed. Based on this feedback, the sponsors added two new requirements to the mentoring program:

- mentors and protégés had to meet at least once a month, and the date for the next meeting was set at the end of the current meeting, and
- protégés set the agenda for what was to be discussed.

These process changes significantly improved both the satisfaction of participants and the overall effectiveness of the intervention.

Step 4. Evaluating Outcomes: Document Results

Steps 1-3 outline how to establish and use process measures effectively. With them in place, documenting results becomes relatively easy. We begin by restating our belief that measuring behavior changes is the foundation for achieving and demonstrating the more traditional business-related goals. Now we focus on three broad business goals we find most companies espouse:

desteklemek, benimsemek

- winning the war for talent;
- maximizing performance; and
- capturing market share

and match them with various initiatives that promote inclusion and a culture of development, those initiatives we have examined throughout this book.

Winning the War for Talent

- Recruitment (Chapters 1 and 5)
- Advancement/Promotion (Chapters 1, 3, 4, 5 and 8)
- Retention/Turnover (Chapters 1, 5 and 8)

Maximizing Performance

- Efficient on-boarding (Chapters 1 and 5)
- Developmental assignments (Chapters 1, 3, 4 and 5)
- Mentoring (Chapters 4 and 6)
- Productivity (Chapters 1, 3, 4, 5 and 8)

Capturing the Market

- Customer satisfaction (Chapter 8)
- Market share (Chapter 8)

Each of these specific strategies or indicators has positive implications for bottom-line profitability, cost savings and market expansion. Of course, as we discussed earlier in this chapter, drawing a direct cause-effect relationship between any initiative and the bottom-line is difficult. We conclude it is not worth the time and expense. In most companies, all but the most skeptical have accepted the important associations as valid.

For example, an insurance client trained many of its sales representatives in "cultural competencies" related to a specific ethnic group targeted for market penetration. The training focused on awareness and understanding as well as specific behavior and used 360-degree feedback reports to verify the sales reps actually acquired the necessary competencies. At the same time the company began a vigorous advertising campaign in that same ethnic group's language. At the end of the year, there was a significant increase in market share; the business goal was met.

Can the increase in market share be attributed to the cultural competency sales training alone? No, but neither can we attribute it to the ad campaign alone. No one would seriously argue that the market played no role in the increase. Why would anyone want to argue that the inclusive training played no role? The sales force's increased knowledge about the ethnic group, including information about very specific sales behavior, made it easier to close the deals. If the company had wanted to demonstrate more precisely the impact of the cultural awareness training on the increase in market share, it could have separated the sales force into two groups—one that took the training and one that did not, and then compared the sales results of each. It could have followed a similar procedure with regard to the ad campaign. Most of us would have found either process a waste of time and money. We think this company wisely chose not to risk losing potential customers by sending out half its sales force without the necessary tools to succeed. You might also say that decision reflected the company's confidence in the efficacy of the training, as well as of the ad campaign.

The business benefits of inclusion and a culture of development can and should be documented in the same way success is documented in any business initiative: benchmark status, identify goals, measure progress at every phase, make appropriate course corrections, and then tie experience to the business outcomes. The goal is to internalize inclusion and a culture of development as part of every company's overall business strategy.

Unleashing The Potential Of Your Workforce

SORT AND SELECT: A CASE STUDY

Recently, we held a session for twenty high-potentials at a large company. The company's stated purpose for the course was to "ensure diversity in the future," because the company leadership "valued the input of all" and believed "employing the widest range of people" would give them "the broadest potential for innovation." The group of twenty identified for the leadership course consisted of nineteen white men and one white woman.

Early in the discussion, the group was in agreement that the company was fair, especially at the highest levels. They also all believed that they had earned their promotions. This response is not surprising, since all of them had benefited from the existing evaluation and promotion process. In addition, no one, including the Novations facilitators, believed that the twenty people in the room were not qualified or had not earned their current favored positions by hard work and excellent performance.

They were asked this question: How did you get the opportunity to perform well and as a result earn your current position? The person who spoke for the group said, "I earned it by performing well on my last assignment."

How about the position before that? Same response: "I earned it by performing well on the prior opportunity." It was clear that successful performances on assigned projects were key to each participant's attribution for good standing within the company.

At this point, the next question asked was: At the beginning of your tenure here, why were you selected for that first stretch assignment? At that point, you had not performed well for the company. Why you? Their initial response was, Why not me? As we continued to discuss this issue, it became obvious to us that this group of professionals had begun to understand what we were looking for.

Their excellent performance didn't just happen. They weren't born that way. It was engineered, the result of a process of development, beginning with selection for the first stretch assignment and the support that encouraged success with it. The result for the person selected was self-confidence and the desire for more challenges. The response of his or her manager complemented those ambitions: confidence in that person's capability to meet future challenges and a willingness to provide those challenges. A mutually beneficial process of continuous development was put in place, resulting in more stretch assignments and more support, leading to more success and more confidence.

LOST POTENTIAL

Typically, organizational cultures select the few who have the opportunity to excel. It is usually unintentional favoritism that leads to someone's selection for the first breakout opportunity. Others are not consciously excluded, but the outcome still remains the same. If the status quo simply continues on its course, without any conscious intervention, those selected for the process of development are most likely to look and act like those who are making the selections.

In a very real sense, the managers dispensing the plum assignments are fulfilling an inherent promise the organization continuously makes to itself, even if the promise is never stated or even consciously thought through. "I will control the company's risk by giving the opportunity to someone I believe is least likely to fail and most likely to deliver high performance." This willingness to assume low risk and high return from someone untested is most likely to benefit people who represent the majority of the population: "I am willing to believe that person shares many of my formative experiences and values and thus will rise to the occasion, as I did." Then success breeds further success, and before long the prophecy is self-fulfilling.

How does that make the "others" feel? Those who are not perceived to be ambitious are unconsciously left out of the process of development. If they see mostly ambitious white men getting the plum assignments, a few will demand inclusion, but most will simply believe they are unable to have any impact. The natural response of many to this clear, though unspoken, message is: "Why should I give my best efforts to this company?" As a result, many people will never fully engage with the business objectives, let alone reach their potential. In today's intensely competitive market, corporations cannot continue to condone a system that leaves so many employees to languish at low levels of engagement. Frankly, they can't afford to.

By allowing these unconscious selection decisions to continue, a company actually chooses to forgo the potential creativity, energy and hard work of a substantial majority of its employees, without any consideration for what it might be losing. The "others" have not been officially labeled as unqualified, but it doesn't matter; they will never have the opportunity to show their full capabilities. Is this a decision that we realize we've made? No. From the perspective of those who assume the environment is a "meritocracy," it appears that we selected the right people. The low-expectation/high-risk prophecy becomes self-fulfilling.

BREAKING THE CYCLE

We have found that inclusion and a culture of development break open this narrow circle and tap into the talent potential of all employees, encouraging them to engage fully in achieving their company's business objectives. The choice is no longer between the few traditional "go-to" people and a large pool of less qualified others. When all have the same opportunities to develop and grow, the choice is between decisions about qualifications based on narrow and subjective standards—what feels right to me based on my experience—versus decisions based on **clearly defined, business-like standards** that everyone understands, accepts and supports.

To build a culture of development, we start with a clearly defined business case: mobilizing the entire workforce is a critical organizational goal. To achieve the goal, eliminating Negative

Treatment is necessary, but we prefer to focus on the positive: Quality Treatment is the answer. This means developing and communicating clear standards for every person's performance; positioning each person to stretch to and even exceed those standards; and then supporting and reinforcing the new behaviors with constructive and honest feedback.

As you reflect on all we have shared in this book, we ask you to take a minute to think back to a time when you were on the receiving end of Quality Treatment, where someone believed in you, positioned you, guided your efforts, and gave you valuable feedback on your performance. What impact did that have on your overall success? Your career? How did it make you feel? Really focus on the feeling you had when you were in that situation, where support and guidance spurred you on. Maybe you even achieved more than you thought was possible. That special feeling is what brings our message to life in your day-to-day activities. When you think about Quality Treatment in the abstract, it seems easy. It *is* easy, when it comes to people who are like us. Working with someone who is a lot like us isn't very complicated at all; without thinking, we gravitate to those people.

The challenge—the stretch—is to provide Quality Treatment to someone who is not like us, someone who is significantly different in some aspect, whether personality type, background, gender, race or age. Think about the possibility of giving Quality Treatment to that person. Can you imagine yourself creating a situation where that person experiences the same positive feelings you had when you received Quality Treatment? If you take the time to define clearly what you expect, position that person to stretch to the standard and reinforce the effort with constructive feedback, that person will *be* different, and perform better. When you define what is expected, position people to stretch with the stated standards as the objective and reinforce their efforts with constructive feedback, it does and will make a difference. Applying this point of view one-on-one across the company will result in expanding the contributions of a much broader base of employees.

THE PROMISE

What did our twenty junior executives feel about the discussion and its revelations? Their CEO came in at the end of the session and asked what had been most important to them. The resounding choice was the discussion about the process of development. They said, "How the organization looks in five years is up to us, and we're going to make sure it looks and is different. We're making a commitment to do what we can to create a culture that develops all potential and makes sure everyone has a chance to excel.

It is our hope that this book, which represents our experiences in many companies across the globe, with employees at every level, has opened your eyes to new possibilities for maximizing your own performance, the performance of your employees and the performance of your company overall. We've shared specific strategies that we have found to be effective again and again, in very different companies and across very different cultures. We can't and won't tell you what to do. You have to decide exactly what steps you want to take when you return to work, because only you know your particular work environment. If providing Quality Treatment to everyone appears to be an impossible task, we ask you to consider our experience. We have found that, once a culture of development becomes your organization's culture, managing talent actually gets easier.

All of us are on a journey of self-discovery, engaged in continuous learning, so the experiences here are intended to stimulate thinking about what's possible, not intended to dictate the one absolute way of doing things. We hope you will be inspired to create new ways of thinking and acting, and new strategies and initiatives based on measurable outcomes, because we firmly believe that an inclusive culture of development will bring about both the most satisfying professional experiences for the widest range of people and the best business results for the organization overall.

Bibliography

Alter, Perry, and Blake Lowry. "Ok, Now I'm Confused: Is My 360° Feedback Process Good or Bad?" *HR.com*, March 29, 2003.

Buckingham, Marcus, and Curt Coffman. *First, Break All the Rules: What the World's Greatest Managers Do Differently.* New York: Simon & Schuster, 1999.

Cattell, Raymond B. *Abilities: Their Structure, Growth, and Action.* Boston: Houghton-Mifflin, 1971.

Cobbs, Price M. *My American Life: From Rage to Entitlement.* New York: Atria Books, 2005.

Cobbs, Price M., and Judith L. Turnock. *Cracking the Corporate Code: The Revealing Success Stories of 32 African-American Executives.* New York: AMACOM, 2003.

Collins, Jim. *Good to Great: Why Some Companies Make the Leap…And Others Don't.* New York: HarperCollins, 2001.

Drucker, Peter. *Management Challenges for the 21st Century.* New York: HarperBusiness, 2001.

Dweck, Carol. *Self Theories: Their Role in Motivation, Personality and Development.* Philadelphia: Psychology Press, 2000.

Ericsson, K. Anders, and Neil Charness. *"Expert Performance: Its Structure and Acquisition." American Psychologist,* 49(8) (1994): 725–747.

Eysenck, Hans J. "Intelligence Assessment: A Theoretical and Experimental Approach." *British Journal of Educational Psychology,* 37 (1967): 81–98.

Fishman, Ted C. *China, Inc.: How the Rise of the Next Superpower Challenges America and the World.* New York: Scribner, 2005.

Galton, F. *Hereditary Genius.* London: Macmillan, 1969.

Greenough, William T., and Janice M. Juraska. "Experience-induced Changes in Brain Fine Structure: Their Behavioral Implications." In M. E. Hahn, C. Jensen, & B. C. Dudek (eds.), *Development and Evolution of Brain Size: Behavioral Implications.* New York, Academic Press, 1979, 295–320.

Greenough, William T., Neal J. Cohen, and Janice M. Juraska. "New Neurons in Old Brains: Learning to Survive?" *Nature Neuroscience,* 2 (1999): 203–205.

Grier, Willlam H., and Price M. Cobbs. *Black Rage.* New York: Basic Books, 1992.

Herrnstein, Richard, and Charles Murray. *The Bell Curve: Intelligence and Class Structure in American Life.* New York: The Free Press, 1994.

Howard, Jeff, and Ray Hammond. "Rumors of Inferiority: The Hidden Obstacles to Black Success." *The New Republic*, 193:5 (September 9, 1985): 17–21.

Howard, Jeffrey P. *From Compliance to Internalization: A Framework for Planning & Mobilizing Diversity Initiatives*. Boston: Novations Group Inc., 2000.

Howard, Jeffrey P. "In the Long Run Inclusion is the Answer." *Profiles in Diversity*, 4:2 (March/April 2002): 31+.

Howard, Jeffrey P. "You Can't Get There from Here: The Need for a New Logic in Education Reform." *Daedalus: Journal of the American Academy of Arts and Sciences*, 124:4 (Fall 1995): 85–92.

Howard, Jeffrey P. *Manage Inclusion: Orchestrate Positions and Build Dispositions*. Boston: Novations Group Inc., 1995.r

Hurston, Zora Neale. *Their Eyes Were Watching God*. New York: J.B. Lippincott, Inc., 1937.

Jensen, A.R. *The g Factor: The Science of Mental Ability*. Westport, CT: Praeger, 1988.

Jensen, Arthur. "How Much Can We Boost I.Q. and Scholastic Achievement?" *Harvard Educational Review*, 39 (February, 1969): 1–123.

Kay, Ira, and Bruce Pfau. "Does 360-degree Feedback Negatively Impact Company Performance?" *HR Magazine*, 47:6 (June 2002): 54+.

Kelman, Herbert C., and V. Lee Hamilton. *Crimes of Obedience: Toward a Social Psychology of Authority and Responsibility.* New Haven: Yale University Press, 1989.

Lawler, Edward E. "The Folly of Forced Ranking." *Strategy + Business*, 28 (2002): 28–32.

Magee, David. *Turnaround: How Carlos Ghosn Rescued Nissan.* New York: HarperCollins, 2003.

Morrison, Toni. *Song of Solomon.* New York: Knopf, 1977.

Rucci, Anthony J., Steven P. Kirn, and Richard T. Quinn. "The Employee-Customer-Profit Chain at Sears." *Harvard Business Review*, 76:1 (1998): 82.

Steele, Claude. "Thin Ice: 'Stereotype Threat' and Black College Students." *The Atlantic Monthly*, 284:2 (August, 1999): 44-47, 50–54

Thomas, David A., and John J. Gabarro. *Breaking Through: The Making of Minority Corporate Executives in Corporate America.* Boston: Harvard Business School Press, 1999.

Yeung, Arthur K, and Bob Berman. "Adding Value Through Human Resources: Reorienting Human Resource Measurement to Drive Business Performance." *Human Resource Management*, 36:3 (Fall 1997): 321–335.

Index

The letter following a page number indicates a figure.